N⦸ B.S.

GUIDE TO

BRAND-BUILDING
BY DIRECT RESPONSE

THE ULTIMATE

CREATING & PROFITING
FROM A
POWERFUL
BRAND

WITHOUT BUYING IT

—— **Dan S. Kennedy** ——

with Forrest Walden & Jim Cavale
—————— OF IRON TRIBE FITNESS ——————

and Special Guest Chapters from WITHDRAWN

DAVE DEE: Chief Marketing Strategist, GKIC

BILL GOUGH: Insurance Industry Marketing Expert

NICK NANTON & J.W. DICKS: Celebrity Branding Agency

STEVE ADAMS: Retail Business Development Expert

And an Exclusive Interview with

MARK VICTOR HANSEN: Co-Creator, *Chicken Soup for the Soul*

Ep
Entrepreneur
PRESS®

Publisher: Entrepreneur Press
Cover Design: Andrew Welyczko
Production and Composition: Eliot House Productions

This publication is designed to provide accurate and authoritative
information in regard to the subject matter covered. It is sold with the
understanding that the publisher is not engaged in rendering legal,
accounting, or other professional services. If legal advice or other
expert assistance is required, the services of a competent professional
person should be sought.

Library of Congress Cataloging-in-Publication Data
Kennedy, Dan S., 1954–
    No B.S. brand-building by direct-response: the ultimate no holds
barred plan to creating and profiting from a powerful brand without
buying it/Dan S. Kennedy with Forrest Walden and Jim Cavale.
      pages cm.
    ISBN-13: 978-1-59918-533-0 (pbk.)
    ISBN-10: 1-59918-533-4
    1. Branding (Marketing) 2. Small business—Management. I. Title.
    HF5415.1255.K46 2014
    658.8′27--dc23

                                2013042630

Printed in the United States of America

18 17 16 15 14   10 9 8 7 6 5 4 3 2 1

Contents

How this Book Will Transform Your Thinking about Your Business and Your Brand

by Dave Dee, Chief Marketing Stategist, GKIC

W hat if a lot of, maybe even everything, you've thought about brand is wrong? Or at least wrong for you?

If you've been thinking of branding as a mystical, magical game-changer that would lift your business from ordinary worth to stratospheric value, this book will transform your thinking and put you on a more practical path. If you've been thinking of branding as a cure for all that ails, this book will transform your thinking and provide action remedies you can use immediately. If you've been suffering brand envy and worrying that owning a powerful brand may be way beyond your reach, this book will transform your thinking and empower you to win even if you're a David up against Goliaths.

One of the core marketing principles developed by Dan Kennedy, which we teach GKIC Members, is that brand-building should be a happy by-product of direct marketing—not purchased outright. This book is a fountain of how-to information and great case history examples drawn from that core principle. GKIC, incidentally, if you don't already know, is an amazing organization of and for marketing-oriented entrepreneurs, small-business owners, private practice professionals, and sales professionals throughout the United States and more than 20 other countries, providing unique information, training, coaching, networking, and support. You can learn more and take advantage of a free offer on page 261.

A Practical Footing

There are two questions we ask entrepreneurs and small-business owners to answer:

1. What is the chief objective of your advertising and marketing?
2. Can you actually afford that chief objective?

A lot of business owners get sold on the idea of getting their name out there. Visibility. Name recognition. Community or marketplace awareness. It's an idea that dates back a very, very long way, to a time when there were lots of towns with only one or even no hardware store, clothing store, dentist, car repair shop, so when one opened up, announcing its presence created quite a stir. Today's marketplace is obviously a lot different. It's hard today to think of a shortage of just about anything in just about any place. Paying for advertising and marketing so you can announce your existence and get your name out there can now be a costly exercise!

If you say that your chief objective in advertising and marketing is to get your name out there and let everybody know who you are, what you do, and where you are and to create name or brand identity and recognition, I may agree, depending on your business, that it's a wonderful objective— *if you can afford it.*

A lot of traditional brand-building you see and might be tempted to copy is done by very well-financed entities with very deep pockets and lots of patience. These examples are dangerous to you, if you copy their strategies without also having their money.

Once they come to grips with the kind of capital investment needed to build a brand from scratch, most businesspeople throw up their hands in surrender. Many who stubbornly or ignorantly plow forward with brand-building on a limited budget find their pockets pretty quickly emptied without having made the impact they'd hoped for and needed to make their business profitable going forward. The blunt truth is that most new business startups and most small businesses that their owners want to grow and expand do not *need* brand identity or recognition, at least not yet. It's a bit like the person who starts a new company and blows his money on fancy offices in a prime location, stuffed with new furniture, then has no money left for advertising. He didn't need all that to start with. He could have begun in a dowdy office with used furniture, or in no office at all. What he needed most and needed immediately is what businesses need most: paying customers, to create profits.

Maybe that seems obvious. If it does, maybe you'd be surprised by how many people pour money and energy into becoming known instead of making money. It happens a lot.

I'm a magician, mostly retired now in favor of my work in marketing. But let me tell you about the most famous magician and the most famous brand ever built in magic: Houdini. It's so well known that there's even a wine cork remover product named The Houdini, and the brand also deconstructed into a generic reference, i.e., pulling a houdini. Houdini originally made himself known town by town, city by city at a time of very limited media. But what he didn't do was make becoming famous his chief objective. He needed to make money. Into each market he went, where he put on a publicity stunt—early on, getting handcuffed and jailed by the local police in the local jail and escaping, and at the same time that story made news, he plastered the town with handbills advertising a show for which tickets could be purchased. As his reputation grew and his brand name become known, he did bigger stunts and even more advertising to promote bigger and more profitable shows. This process built his brand with zero direct capital investment—as a by-product of making money.

How to Think about This and How NOT to Think about This

When you think about your brand, you think about you and your product or business and all your virtues and benefits. You stand in front of the mirror, look at yourself, and say, "Hey, I'm smart and valuable and good-looking, too!" You think about what you want to be known for and what you want your brand to symbolize.

When you want to make money, you think about who has money they might be willing to spend—a target market, and what they would be interested in buying with it—which guides a message.

One of the biggest and deadliest marketing mistakes, especially by people with brand on their minds, is trying to appeal to everybody. "Everybody" is a whole lot of people. It's a huge ocean with big waves, not very nice to small rowboats. Few business owners have big enough boats. The best answer is not waiting endlessly until you can build a bigger boat or being held back forever because you can't. Successful people never let their available resources control them—they work with strategies that can be used with the resources they have.

For Money Now, Focus on the Best, Most Obtainable Customer, Not the Idealized Brand

It's cool to want to build a famous and dynamic brand that people respect, care about, buzz about. It's a grand ambition. And you can create it. But you need to pay the light bill.

At the GKIC Fast Start Implementation Boot Camps (www.DanKennedy.com/bootcamp) we spend a lot of time on what you can do right now. Almost every business owner can identify a small, manageably sized target market or prospect group for which his products or services are ideally matched, and then he can figure out—often with our help—how to directly reach out just to them. He can get response from them, make profitable sales to them, and in the process, build his brand 10, 50, 100 people at a time, in much the same way Houdini did it, one town at a time. We have a lot of technology and tools today to speed and expand that process that Houdini didn't have and would undoubtedly have kid-in-a-candy store enthusiasm for, but I'm confident he'd still want to make money as his chief objective.

Target Market Thinking

Again, at those Fast Start Implementation Boot Camps, we tackle key questions about your best prospective customers. Who are they and what might they have in common? Gender, age, geographic area, income, politics, interests? What motivates them? What is a big frustration of theirs your product or service solves, a secret or stated fear you can ease, a great desire you can help them achieve? The more complete and exact this picture you have of your ideal or avatar customer, the better able you are to develop a very persuasive message for them and attract them to you. If you would like help with developing your Customer Avatar, there is training from the Implementation Boot Camps available free at www. DanKennedy.com. It will only take you about 30 minutes online to develop your Avatar.

I Know, You'd RATHER Think about Your Brand

Obviously you bought this book because it promised to be about brand-building. It is, and we'll get there, but we are going to get there by a different road than you probably imagined!

Here's a brand you know—Snapple®. You may very well know at least one of its slogans: the best-tasting stuff on earth. You've seen TV commercials. You see it on your grocery store shelves. Maybe you drink it and enjoy it. It's certainly a big brand in the soft drink category, where it is very, very difficult to go up against the well-established major brand names and win some space on the shelf and support from customers.

What you may not know is that Snapple® was not launched or built with the kind of brand advertising you see for it now. The makers of Snapple® were barely crawling around, not even toddling upright, when a very strange and lucky thing happened. The radio commentator Rush Limbaugh was relatively early in his rise, and having a lot of trouble convincing any brand-name companies to advertise with him. The big brand boys feared negative backlash because of Limbaugh's outspoken conservative opinions and doubted that his kind of talk show could drive retail sales. Rush noticed Snapple®, determined it was a very young, small, regional brand with very limited distribution, and thought it would be a great test of his ability to spark widespread interest in a new and unknown brand. So he did a crazy thing. Without selling them advertising or even telling them he was giving them advertising, he began advertising Snapple® on his program as if they were an advertiser!

Suddenly supermarket managers were awash in people demanding Snapple®. Sales soared where it was available, and requests from supermarket and convenience store chains and operators from all over the country, including areas they'd never yet tried getting distribution, poured into Snapple's offices. The executives scratched their heads at their mysterious good fortune, until they discovered "the Limbaugh experiment" being conducted for them. They then became a real, regular advertiser and built their brand and national distribution rapidly. Limbaugh started and they, for a time, stuck with very simple direct-response style advertising: talking about a problem—being bored with ordinary sodas and beverages, promising a new and different product, and telling people to go to their local store to get it, and if it wasn't there, to demand it.

Don't miss the point here of a target market. For Snapple® to make itself a famous and exciting brand for everybody, known as Coca-Cola® or Pepsi® are known, would have required an ocean of money and a cat's supply of lifetimes. But to become a famous brand just amongst loyal Limbaugh listeners could be achieved in a short time with limited, narrowly focused resources—in this case, one audience reached directly with one media. This is why Dan Kennedy says: Audience is everything!

How I Raised Myself to Success by Thinking about Customers, Not about Brand

As I said, in my prior career, I was a professional magician. I didn't mention that I was a struggling, almost starving magician when I first heard Dan Kennedy speak and offer his *Magnetic Marketing System®*, now GKIC's flagship product. At the time, I was trying to become known, and I was struggling to book three shows a month. After switching to a direct marketing approach, I quickly leapt to 30 shows a month. Within one year, I had totally turned my income and career around. That's when I began to package up, sell, and teach what I had learned about effectively marketing myself to other magicians. (The packaging and selling of know-how is called "information marketing." You can learn more about it at www.dankennedy/infomarketing.) Now, here's what's important about my target market then, other magicians.

On the surface, these magicians I wanted to sell my business course to wanted to learn how to book more shows and make more money. But what they secretly, more deeply desired most was to show all the people telling them they'd never make a living as a professional magician that they were wrong.

This business grew fast and was very profitable and successful, and it made me a well-known figure and brand name in the magic field. It's from there that I went on to a bigger business in training and coaching entrepreneurs. I did not worry about building my brand; I set about creating products and sales messages that interested a target audience, to make money. The brand-building just tagged along. Were I doing it all over again today, I'd probably be more conscious of the brand-building, but I would still ask it to ride in the back seat while up front I focused on driving profits.

By the End of this Book . . .

If you bought this book because you know the Dan Kennedy brand, the No B.S. brand, the GKIC brand, or the *Entrepreneur* brand, or all of them, you probably have a high trust in them and have entered these pages confident of having a valuable experience and of having profitable actions to take afterward. In case you don't have that kind of familiarity with us, you may find it helpful to read the abbreviated descriptions of Dan's experience, the other contributors, and GKIC on pages 251 to 254 before beginning.

By the end of this book, you will *know* what it takes to *use* our core principle: brand-building should be a happy by-product of direct marketing—not purchased outright. You will have met great entrepreneurs and gotten an insider's look at case histories to understand how they have used this principle in practical ways.

Now, at the start of this book, all you need is a reasonably open and curious mind.

DAVE DEE is a professional magician, author of *The Psychic Salesman/Selling System*, and an accomplished sales trainer, speaker and entrepreneurial coach, successful information marketer, and Chief Marketing Strategist of GKIC. He can be reached at www.DanKennedy.com.

CHAPTER 1

The Golden Opportunity and the Harsh Reality of Owning a Brand

by Dan S. Kennedy

"Differentiate or die."

—JACK TROUT

I am often introduced as "The Millionaire Maker," a nod to the fact that my advice and marketing strategies have lifted hundreds and hundreds, if not thousands and thousands, of people new to business, people with ideas brought to market, owners of established but ordinary businesses, and self-employed professionals to seven-figure incomes and to million and multimillion-dollar wealth. I am also often introduced as "The Professor of Harsh Reality," which is more in keeping with my main brand, which I'll talk about a bit later. This, because I famously rip to shreds illusion, delusion, treasured beliefs, conventional "wisdom," and industry norms and expose charlatans and fakers and theorists. This sometimes makes me unwelcome, and it's possible that will be the case here, if you have treasured beliefs, illusions, or delusions about the magical power of a brand.

On the surface, asking <u>me</u> to write a book on brand-building, as *Entrepreneur* did, seemed odd to me and to many who know me well, with whom I shared the mission. Hiring a heretic to pastor a church. I am a very vocal, near constant critic of big, brand-name companies and their huge expenditures on brand or image advertising. I am incessantly cautioning small-business owners, entrepreneurs, and private practice operators not to emulate the behavior of the big brand advertisers, due to their very different agendas as well as the emperors with no sense in their boardrooms. The potential to brand-build your way to bankruptcy is very real.

I make fun of corporate goofiness, like the pink bunny with the drum that everybody knows but more than half of consumers queried attach it to the wrong band of battery, or the infamous Taco Bell stuffed dog that starred in months of commercials (replacing the food) only to produce a decline in sales, or the fortunes spent tweaking logos and meaningless slogans. When I was writing this book, *USA Today* actually had the unbridled corporate ego to trumpet its new logo—a big blue dot, by the way—as front page *news*, as if anybody but its designer and his mother cared. Bone-headed corporate CEOs routinely pour millions into brand symbols, logos, and slogans, and issue pompous press releases, even hold press conferences to announce their foolishness. It is routine folly to grossly exaggerate the significance and value of brands.

Of course, there *are* plenty of iconic, powerhouse brands worth fortunes. In entertainment, James Bond, Batman, Superman, The Avengers, Disney. In food, Campbell's Soup and Coca-Cola. Name a category, you can certainly name both corporate and personal brands that have sustained magnetic power. I've never denied that. I've just said that the way many have been built is not by throwing oceans of money into buying recognition, awareness, and familiarity, as most peddlers of brand-building theory and of ad media would have you believe. Also, that there's no warranty of inevitability of brand power or value either.

In autos, Rambler was once a good brand. So was Pontiac. It even owned a craze for a time, the Pontiac Trans-Am, made famous by Burt Reynolds in *Smokey and the Bandit*. Oldsmobile, the symbol of having made it, but not wanting to be a show-off. They're all gone. Zeroed out. One of the classic cars I drive around in is a 1972 AMC Javelin SST, then a very hot car (see below). Now, people ask: What is *that*? And often, when I say it was made by American Motors, people ask what that was.

More people know Jeep, of course, and today it is a valuable brand. But it twice flirted with extinction. The Jeep in the photo above is my restored 1986 Jeep Wagoneer, which I bought, on impulse, of all places, out of an Orvis catalog. And I felt fine doing so because Orvis is a trusted brand to me. If you're unfamiliar with them, they are a long established catalog company, selling everything from apparel to hunting and fishing excursions. Orvis shirts, slacks, and a favorite leather jacket hang in my closet. If they say this is a well-restored classic car, I believe them.

Increasingly, a brand is important to consumers—and therefore valuable—in categories of goods or services over-cluttered with competing choices and like or identical pricing, as a shortcut to decision, desperately needed in an over-busy life. Yet, this value and importance can, in some cases, be long-standing, as with, say, Campbell's Soup or Bounty paper towels (you know, the quicker picker upper), but it can also lose its grip, as, say, Holiday Inns, or it can go from firm grip on consumer consciousness to utter oblivion, as, say, Timex or Dr. Spock (once THE name in advice for parents) or Firestone (a brand so weakened its name was even removed from its own PGA tournament held at the country club bearing its name). Brands can be important, until they aren't.

Brand as a holy grail or as a panacea for what ails a business—I buy neither and rail against both. And I strongly caution against pouring capital into a brand, per se.

Yet, here I am, adding a book on brand-building to my stable of No B.S. books. When I took it on, I had my doubts it could be done without B.S. But, then again, I have had and have a lot of clients with very valuable brands they grew without having to pour oceans of money into them. That is what this book is about, in terms of strategy and tactics: **getting a great brand—free**. That makes this book radically different from any other books or advice in this category. Everything else about brands is piled high at one end of the library. This little book sits by itself, at the far, opposite end.

A Brand Atheist. A Brand Believer.

I am fundamentally a <u>direct</u> marketing guy. That means I want to be able to accurately, ruthlessly measure a money return on each and every dollar invested, preferably quickly. No ambiguity. No vague idea of gain by awareness. Show me the money. It also means I want <u>direct</u> response. Outreach that brings a customer to the door, credit card in hand. Big, valuable brands can and are created as free by-products of this kind of direct-marketing activity, including many owned by past or present clients of mine. Weight Watchers, a famous brand built with no brand-building advertising. Guthy-Renker's Proactiv®, an $800-million-a-year business with a brand worth at least five times that much, created, built and sustained without brand or image advertising—one I'm proud to have made some small contributions to from time to time. Priceline.com, originally raised from scratch by hard-core direct-response radio advertising created and managed by my colleague and friend, Fred Catona at Bulldozer Media. The fast-growth software, Infusionsoft, which you'll read about later in the book. These are all valuable brands that *weren't* bought.

There is one brand I know more about than any other, and we'll start this book's journey with it . . .

This odd photo represents a powerful and valuable brand.

It was first used in 1993, and has since been in perpetual and proliferate use, adorning literature, book covers, catalogs, newsletters, websites, even a bobblehead doll.

It's a (much younger) me, on a rented albino bull—the bull itself a celebrity, having appeared in two Disney films and at countless trade show booths and shopping center grand openings. Its name is Tiny. Mine is Dan Kennedy. And I'm known for being the "No B.S." guy. The actual business logo representing that brand concept is this:

This brand logo has adorned apparel, caps, wall posters, mousepads, jigsaw puzzles, toys, pens, flashlights, as well as books, newsletters, websites, and more.

These brand images mean something to those they mean something to. Maybe you are one of those people, maybe not (yet). But maybe its obvious meaning attracted you to or interested you in this very book. No B.S. is pretty straightforward. It means blunt, unmitigated, unqualified truth. It's said that there is a small market for the truth, and I have found that to be the truth—but it is a small and mighty market: a rabid, appreciative, and loyal audience. Being a truth-teller is not the easiest road to prosperity to travel, but it has proved itself a very reliable and rewarding one.

This Gets to the Question: What, Exactly, Is a Brand?

In the old West, it was an identifying mark burned onto livestock with a fire-heated iron to thwart rustlers and cattle thieves. In similar fashion, businesses and individuals try to mark themselves with a distinct brand and embed that brand in the minds of the public at large or a specific, targeted population, to thwart copycatting and commoditization. It can be said about a very distinctive comedian, like the late Steven Wright, or Andrew Dice Clay, or my friend Joan Rivers, that they have a particular *brand of* humor. Serious students or even great fans of comedy would likely recognize a Steven Wright or Joan Rivers joke if written out on a 3-by-5 card. For a couple of decades, Cadillac was so branded on the public brain as the symbol of excellence and status that the phrase "The Cadillac of . . ." was used to describe (and nearly co-brand) all sorts of non-auto products. *"This, madam, is the Cadillac of vacuum cleaners," said the door-to-door salesman to the happy homemaker.*

A brand can be a representation of a philosophy or a philosophical position, a reason to do business with a person or entity, an instant message that communicates what a person or product or business is about. It can be aggressive or gentle, bold or subtle. It can represent the values or aspirations of a community of consumers or followers. It can be represented by a name in distinct typeface like Disney's or IBM's or by a distinctive image like Apple's or the Playboy bunny. Many great brands are actually ideas, like *Chicken Soup for the Soul* (see pages 231 to 234), or another of my created brands:

This is a philosophy and lifestyle brand. It marries two great aspirations. A whole lot of people would like to be rich. If you doubt it, watch the number of people buying Power Ball tickets as giant jackpots mount. And a whole lot of people like thinking of themselves as renegades, and many more would love to be, if they dared or felt they could afford the luxury. A lot of successful brands are aspirational, like Cadillac and Martha Stewart.

A lot of what people believe about brand value, based on academic theory, Madison Avenue ad agencies and their frequent conning of big, dumb companies' leaders out of shareholders' money, and simple assumption that brand automatically equals power is just B.S., piled high. A lot of money is wasted by small-business owners and entrepreneurs on brand-building strategies that mimic those of big, dumb companies. A brand can be a big drain into which money gets poured. Kind of like a yacht or a California divorce. Or, a brand can be a valuable asset, with much of that value measurable. Very accurate appraisal of brand equity occurs through brand licensing. Personalities like Gene Simmons (KISS) and Martha Stewart have been paid hundreds of millions of dollars to attach their names to all manner of products. There are, for example, KISS condoms and KISS caskets—as Gene puts it, brand licensing money made from the cradle to the grave.

A brand can be important to consumers in different ways. It can, as I said before, help cut through marketplace clutter and chaos and sheer quantity of noise, to make choosing within a category easy and efficient. It can often be a guarantee of consistency, of a certain kind or level of experience, so that the consumer can know in advance what to expect, and what not to expect. It can provide pride of ownership and status; it can enable somebody to be in "the cool kids' club;" it can stroke one's ego: *I am because I own*. It can validate a person's values or aspirations: *I am a good mother because I serve this brand of food*. It can satisfy at an emotional level, as with nostalgia brands.

We will explore everything a brand can and can't be and can and can't do for you or your business in this book. Most importantly, we will dispel B.S., and we will be clear about *wise* strategies to develop and build brand identity and equity without direct investment.

I have never spent a cent on outright brand advertising of any sort, yet within my chosen target markets my personal brand is strong—meaning, people know me, know what I'm about, and know what to expect when dealing with me. And my business brands are well recognized by customers, clients, readers, subscribers, and the fields in which I conduct business. The members of the organization built by me and around me, GKIC, which publishes the *No B.S. Marketing Letter*, identify with and have affinity for the No B.S. brand. In fact, many own logo apparel, desk ornaments, and various items linked to that brand. What might surprise some is that I have no interest in *everybody* recognizing these brands. Nor in just anybody recognizing them. I have very deliberately made myself what I call a famous person nobody's ever heard of—except the select audience that is of the highest value to me and best fit with me. One of the great myths of brand-building is that a brand's value is proportionate to the raw numbers of those who know it. That can be true, but it isn't always true.

Business and marketing decisions, especially those about your brands, need to follow a linear path:

Principle > Strategies > Tactics

Great brands stand for something. Sam Walton knew exactly what he wanted Walmart to be when it grew up, and could clearly enunciate a handful of core principles. Ray Kroc had three principles on which to govern the growth of McDonald's. The extremely successful celebrity-entrepreneur Kathy Ireland, who spoke at one of GKIC's annual Marketing and Moneymaking SuperConferences^{SM}, explained there the key principles behind her brand, which now supports thousands of products and drives a multi-million-dollar empire. Walt Disney put his business's number-one principle into its slogan and Unique Selling Proposition, something of a feat: *The* Happiest Place On Earth. The over-arching principle of all my work, represented by my brand, is truth-telling. Absolute, unvarnished, bare naked truth-telling. Brands backed by principle tend to outsell, outperform, and outlast brands that aren't. If you stand for nothing, you can be felled by just about anything.

From principle come strategies. Each of the above examples followed that path. If you obtain and read the autobiographies and biographies of these men and women and of other great entrepreneurs who've built powerful personal or business brands, you will find that each of their few chief principles drove a plethora of strategic decisions.

I'll use myself as an example here, and rattle off a sampling of strategic decisions mandated by my chief principle, in no particular order:

- I have been selective, discriminating, and deliberate in the clients, customers, members, and fans I've sought and deliberately, overtly repelled others—so that I could be a truth-teller at all times, in every piece of work (book, newsletter, seminar, etc.) without worry over who I might offend or what sale or revenue I might lose by not sugar-coating or walking on tiptoes on the thin ice of political correctness.

- I have focused on entrepreneurial business owners, business builders, and CEOs rather than larger, perhaps more lucrative corporate clients—because I understand and admire the determined entrepreneur but often question the very sanity and competence of corporate executives.

- I've never sold or permitted anyone else to sell anything to my clientele, members, followers without at least a 30-day unconditional guarantee—because if any individual feels they were not told the truth about a product or service, I do not want them feeling stuck with something "false" to them.

- I have been personally transparent with my members and clientele. For example, I have written and publicly spoken about my now long, long ago bankruptcy; my long ago heavy boozing; and I use my marketing misfires and flops as well as my successes as teaching examples. Contrary to the caution that business and politics don't mix, the folks who follow me have no doubt about where I stand on political matters.

Just to give you a couple non-Dan examples:

Farm-to-table restaurants are based on a certain obvious principle. This governs strategic choices about physical location, menu items and food sources and vendors, and tactical decisions about price. Ralph Nader's quixotic presidential campaigns (that made him a bestselling author, popular speaker, media personality—and quite wealthy) centered on being against corporate influence in politics, and this principle governed strategy about who he would and could not take donations or other support from, then tactical decisions about how he could and would raise money and finance campaigns. Bill Cosby determined he never wanted to do anything his young daughter or aging mother would be embarrassed to hear or watch. This principle governed strategic career choices about agents and managers, film and TV projects, down to the tactical choices of jokes, comedy material, and words he would and would not use.

Often, acting in a way that contradicts principle severely damages or ruins a personal or corporate brand. President Bush No.1 was, in the short term, virtually ruined by his failure to honor his "Read my lips—NO new taxes" pledge. A big-time TV preacher, Jimmy Swaggert, a moralist, never recovered from his public scandal involving under-age prostitutes. (For somebody like a rap music star or mogul, the same scandal might be helpful.) Disney has carefully, tentatively negotiated and expanded the serving of alcoholic beverages in select places and at certain times in its parks—something antithetical to Walt's principles for the parks (although Walt personally was a drinker). Strategies that contradict principle are equally perilous. Pierre Cardin and Oleg Cassini were once very elite and exclusive fashion brands, but by extremely aggressive and indiscriminate licensing, including several different price levels and distribution channels for the same category of items—like sunglasses in boutiques at $500.00 but also in department stores at $50.00 and in discount stores for $19.95—their value was destroyed. The minute you can buy a cheaply made handbag with the Birkin brand on it, in unlimited quantity, at Target, the end for Birkin will be near. Disney licensed out the operation of its retail stores in shopping malls and gave up managerial control of the Florida community it created, Celebration, and lived to regret both strategic decisions as damaging to its brand. (It remedied the matter of the stores. It was too late to re-take control of Celebration). With 20/20 hindsight, there is only one strategic decision I've personally made in my own businesses that I consider damaging to my brand, and I'm embarrassed to say I repeated it and made fundamentally the same mistake twice. It was at odds with Principle.

Just as linking Principle to Strategies is powerful, de-linking them is dangerous.

Day by Day, Hour by Hour, Choice by Choice
We Weave Strands of Fabric That Become
the Cape of a Super-Hero
Or the Shroud of a Disgraced Pariah

Finally, we can get to tactics. This is too often where businesspeople begin or hurry, even race, to implementation. Advertising and marketing content, media, and process decisions are very often made with little or no regard to a principle that governs strategy. Entrepreneurs are often "Ready, Fire, Then Aim" people. Entrepreneurs are often operating under extreme time or financial pressure. The temptations to make tactical moves without full consideration of them against strategies set by principle is difficult to resist. Often, we don't even slow down enough to recognize that is what we're doing!

Martha Stewart risked great brand damage when she took Kmart as her first major retail partner. It was a simple tactical act: They were there with money and no one else was, and they had—at the time—enormous distribution power. She made a similar, apparently money- and immediacy-driven decision when she broke with Macy's and did a huge deal with J.C. Penney, creating a triangle of messy, expensive, and hazardous litigation, ill will, and bad PR. Pharmaceutical companies helped themselves tremendously when they became direct-to-consumer advertisers in print media and on TV, when they copied a favorite tactic of late-night infomercials and hired and showcased celebrity spokespersons, a practice they continue to use. Sleep Number Beds began as a pure direct marketer and built their brand by direct-response advertising, but then made a tactical decision to open and operate their own local, brick-and-mortar retail locations (as opposed to distributing through other retailers or remaining a pure direct marketer), a decision that appears to be working out well for them. It has not worked out well at all for a number of other direct marketers, including brands like The Sharper Image and J. Peterman. Iron Tribe Fitness's owners decided to operate the opposite of most gyms, limiting membership to just 300 rather than selling as many memberships as possible, and selling at a very premium price as opposed to the common, cheap fee. This is working out very well for them. A friend of mine self-published his health book, chooses not to sell it via Amazon or any other bookseller or in any ebook form (where it would probably bring from $4.00 to $9.00), sells it direct to consumers by direct mail only (at a $45.00 price), and has sold nearly 250,000 books at a nice profit. These are all tactical decisions. There are so many tactical options to consider that it's vital to have a fixed basis for evaluating them—such as Strategies based on Principle.

The brands I built and the relationship they and I have with my target market formed the basis for a substantial sale of the company I founded and built, GKIC, to private equity investors, who now own it. It's very rare for an individual author or speaker or thought leader to create a business with real, salable equity. These businesses are mostly income plays, not equity plays. Most are truthfully glorified jobs masquerading as businesses. Not mine. Mine was, in fact, sold twice, first to Bill Glazer, who helmed it with me heavily involved for about ten years, and again to the professional investment group. They valued this company in the tens of millions of dollars. All centered around little ol' me. Why? Because, in my small way, in my niche field, I emulated truly extraordinary builders of brand value like Walt Disney and Hugh Hefner. (See Chapter 17.) I made my personal brand and affiliation with me, and my business brands and involvement with them, about high trust (like Disney) and dynamic aspiration (like Hefner). Within the confines and dictates of principle, I was extremely strategic. You will come away with a better, clearer, deeper understanding of why this approach is so important and how you can use it for any business, product, person, or cause.

I pride myself on pragmatism, so I've made this a very practical book. It lays out a productive path, not an ethereal and theoretical jumble of ideas. But this is also an inspirational book. It shows how you can take your business and make it really mean something to its customers. My co-authors from Iron Tribe Fitness demonstrate this clearly. I hope you find this premise exciting and motivational: the making a business into something that really means something to its customers.

Frankly, *just* selling stuff and making money, even a lot of money, is neither mysterious rocket science nor beyond anyone's reach, because of upbringing, education, resources, or any other common excuse for poor life outcomes. I have a happy relationship with money and like making it and like, a lot more, having it, but just making it never really fascinated me. It now seems mundane. I think it's damnably difficult to sustain creativity and enthusiasm for any business if *all* you're doing with it is exchanging goods or services for money. The building of a powerful brand and a positive relationship with a group of customers to whom your work and your business is important and means something, that is a far more interesting exercise. It is a lie to suggest that, if you do that, plenty of money will automatically follow. Don't believe that for a minute. But it is true that when that is done in concert with the other functions of business, with maximum profits and value as a co-pilot to principle and passion, and sound disciplines of marketing and management applied, it's easier and a great deal more interesting and fulfilling to stack up the pesos.

How Are You to Learn AND IMPLEMENT Brand-Building by Direct Response?

It's possible that the best education is demonstration.

Two of the best practitioners of brand-building by direct response that I've consulted with, coached, and observed closely over the past several years are Forrest Walden and Jim Cavale, developers of a unique franchise concept in the fitness industry. In the next nine chapters, they provide an in-depth show-'n-tell demonstration of exactly how to do it, from startup to local market dominance to national expansion, beginning simply, then becoming incredibly sophisticated. Their chapters are rich with examples, and there is a video extension of every chapter at *www.IronTribeFranchise.com/NoBS*. I'll return after these chapters, to talk about different applications of brand-building by direct response.

One quick caution: Please do not sabotage yourself with the small, provincial, and very unimaginative ". . . but MY business is different" thinking. If that's where your mind is at and will stay, you might as well stop right here, return this book for a refund, and move on. NO business is different. ALL businesses require the attraction and fascination and motivation of customers, and ALL successful businesses thrive by converting at least some of those customers to evangelical advocates. In short, to successful tribalism. Few tribes rise and stay together without a powerful brand to which they have allegiance. In this profound way, ALL businesses are the same—so all the lessons of Iron Tribe apply to all businesses.

Attempting success as an entrepreneur with a closed mind is akin to leaping from an airplane and making the rest of the journey with a closed parachute.

Even the Amish aren't this Amish. In GKIC, studying my methods through the *No B.S. Marketing Letter* and the myriad of other resources and at our conferences, right along with the Iron Tribe guys, there are Amish restaurant owners, furniture manufacturers, wealth managers and financial advisors, inventors, publishers, and other kinds of entrepreneurs proactively borrowing "what works" from wildly diverse sources of ideas, information, and inspiration. Everyone with an open mind!

CHAPTER 2

They Digest Your Marketing Before You Have a Brand

by Jim Cavale

ith Iron Tribe, we knew the mountain we wanted to climb was brand. To have a recognized and understood brand that people felt drawn to and wanted to be part of was our goal. But we did not drive in that exact direction at first. We began by building gyms, not a brand. We began by marketing those gyms, not a brand. We began by selling memberships, not a brand. In the beginning, we just let the brand come along for the ride.

It had been just one year since Forrest Walden and I began franchising our life-changing, Birmingham-based Iron Tribe Fitness brand, and we were finishing up a two-day trip to Charlotte, where we had the chance to coach up our newest franchisees on their pre-opening sales and marketing initiatives.

Before we left town, we decided to visit a mentor who works in the investment banking world. His firm is perched high atop one of the modern skyscrapers located in Charlotte's Uptown district.

As we walked through this new, not-yet-established market for Iron Tribe, a group passing by us suddenly shouted out "Iron Tribe!"

I turned and said, "Yes, the logo on my shirt represents Iron Tribe. How do you know about us?"

A young man emerged from the group and said that he'd seen us building in a couple of different areas in Charlotte, where our gym construction signs had been put up and direct-response advertisements were already running.

Based on what he said, he'd clearly digested our marketing. Which means he was educated and informed on how exactly Iron Tribe provides "LIFE. Changed."

Our initial marketing messages trained him to know that we only have 300 member athlete spots available at the gym opening near him, and if he acts now, he has the chance to join this tribe of athletes that will be established in his backyard and several other places throughout the "Queen City."

Just one of dozens of U.S. markets where we are now developing our Iron Tribe brand.

He and his friends knew these things about Iron Tribe because we set out to clearly communicate them in our advertising and marketing—not just promote a vague idea, slogan, or logo. As direct-response marketers, it seems kind of crazy that we have actually built powerful brand identity. To our clients, our logo *is* known and prized. We didn't get to this point overnight or by directly investing in brand identity.

We've come a long way, from a small group of 30-somethings working out in Forrest's garage to a nationally franchised fitness chain with more than 50 gym territories sold (and counting), just three years later.

It began with one gym built upon a strict dedication to Dan Kennedy's direct-response marketing principles, and it has *evolved* into a brand that people truly want to be a part of, as member athletes, as employee coaches and managers, and as brand ambassador franchise owners.

Heck, it was a direct-response sales letter from Forrest himself that arrived in my mailbox, only to make me feel like I'd be crazy NOT to be a founding member athlete of this brand-new gym called Iron Tribe that was opening around the corner from my house!

I rushed in to become one of the first ever Iron Tribe member athletes, and my life was so transformed that I was moved to change my entire entrepreneurial trajectory.

So just a few months after Forrest started this new Iron Tribe Fitness gym concept, I approached him with aspirations of partnering to bring Iron Tribe to the world. It was a big idea that might have seemed insane to most people at that time, but not to him. That's the very reason he started it in the first place—to make a life-changing impact on the world, one life at a time.

Three years later, we are living out our dream, establishing a brand that is much bigger than ourselves, growing a nationwide franchise model with world impact aspirations, and ultimately, continuing to make this impact one person at a time with a systematized business model that has proven scalable.

How did we get here so fast? How can we maintain this growth pace at such a rapid rate? What makes us think that we have an actual brand and not just one of the latest fitness fads?

Great questions.

There are several different paths I could take in approaching each, but there would be one common denominator in each of those answers—Iron Tribe is a brand that is built upon a solid base of direct-response marketing systems.

Dan Kennedy once told us that "those who choose to grow their business from the beginning, with a foundation in direct-response marketing, will simply be more agile and so do the things that the big companies won't do and can't do, even though they want to. And should you become a big boy with direct response at your core, you have the chance to spread your tentacles around the entire globe."

The majority of small-businessmen have it completely backwards when it comes to building a brand-marketing platform that attracts new clients like a cult following. Everyone wants it, but most are not willing to do what it takes to get there.

Instead of starting with direct response or even using it whatsoever, most businesses tend to act as if they are already an established brand, wasting real estate on their ad space with oversized logos and clever slogans that the market doesn't even notice.

This is a result of the masses copying the masses. Which of course, is always a no-no. My father raised me on the principle of watching what everyone else does and doing the opposite, and that rule certainly applies here.

Don't get me wrong, your brand and your logo can eventually stand for something. But first you have to raise your logo up like a child and earn it some respect.

Customers, Sales, Revenues, and Profits First

This enthusiasm starts with a first step of actually going out there with your new business and getting clients. Then you have to fulfill their orders with an experience that makes them feel good about seeing your business's cost on their bank statement.

Despite what most people would like to think, marketing is much more than hiring a graphic designer who creates a trendy logo and colorful sales brochures, hoping to distribute these pretty materials and watch the cash come pouring into your bank account.

Instead, marketing is the science of getting your message to your market, with a willingness to test multiple messages and medias, and a strict dedication to tracking each of these tests in great detail. These tests produce successes and failures that turn marketing theories into a winning marketing plan. On its back, your brand can evolve.

This success starts with the direct-response formulaic approach, and if you do it right, you can actually earn your brand some respect. Maybe even enough respect to attract loads of new clients who want to be a part of a tribe—to be a part of something bigger than themselves.

Go to IronTribeFranchise.com/NoBS to watch Jim Cavale & Forrest Walden provide commentary on this chapter.

CHAPTER 3

How I Discovered Direct Response

by Forrest Walden

irect response is a different animal.

Most of the advertising you see is not direct response. Much of it is brand-driven advertising, either promoting a brand or, more frequently, reinforcing an already recognized and established brand. Because the majority of all the advertising you see is this kind, you are naturally oriented toward doing that kind of advertising. But if you don't have a brand as established and universally recognized as Ford or Budweiser or Apple or ESPN, it is very dangerous to copy what they and companies like them do. I learned that it is more useful to look at much younger, now known brands that seem to have come out of nowhere and become widely known, like the George Foreman Grill, or even to look at ideas that have become widely known and accepted, like individuals independently buying and flipping real estate properties. These kinds of brands and ideas established themselves by their owners actually selling things.

To get the kind of speed to success and speed to a brand that Jim and I have achieved with Iron Tribe, you have to, in the short term, ignore the brand advertising examples and focus on direct response.

I Answer an "Odd" Ad and I'm Shown the Different Road

I'll never forget the rainy night in November 2002, when I was reading a personal training trade journal and my life was changed forever. Now, of course, I had no idea that my life was about to change or that I was being introduced to direct-response marketing and a new way to think about, market, and grow my business.

My eye was drawn to a quarter-page ad that stood out because it was so different from every other ad in the publication. The other ads were pictorial and graphic, flashy, and visual. Most had sparse, short copy. Big logos. Many made no direct request for any sort of response, instead just showing a product, presenting a company, advertising a brand and its idea. Think Nike® and Just Do It®. This ad stood out like the only red convertible in a funeral procession of black limousines. Or, more like an ugly mutt in the middle of the Westminster Dog Show and its magnificently groomed purebreds on parade. It was plain. Its headline said, "Free Audio Tape Reveals The Ultimate Fitness Marketing Success Secret," then it went on to instruct me to call an 800 number for a free recorded message for more information.

Although I thought this was weird, I felt compelled to call the number and listen to the short three-minute elevator speech. I was further instructed to leave my name and full mailing address so that I could be mailed an audiotape and a free report called "How to Get More Clients in the Next 90 Days Than You Now Get All Year . . . Without Networking, Hard Selling, or Begging for Referrals." I complied with the instructions and went on about my busy life of building my (then) three personal training studios.

Up to that point in my career, my business partner at the time, Aaron Crocker, and I had opened three of our own brick-and-mortar one-on-one personal training locations. While we were growing, getting great results for our clients, and experiencing some good internal referrals, I was unhappy with the results of my external marketing.

I was a fitness guy at heart. I had spent my education and career up to that point learning everything there was to know about helping my clients get into the best shape of their lives. I knew next to nothing about how to attract clients who were predisposed to doing business with me, and I was quickly learning that my glossy oversized image-driven postcards were ineffective and that trying to book appointments with "suspects" and then educating them during the consult process was not working well for me.

This was leading me to sell out of weakness, getting low

> **FOR A DEEPER UNDERSTANDING**
>
> You can see the old, original "ugly ad" that Forrest answered and the entire "Free Report" that he received at www.rapidprofitsystem.com, and you can watch a video of Forrest and Jim Cavale discussing direct response at www.IronTribeFitnessFranchise.com/NoBS.

closing percentages and small average customer contracts—if they even decided to purchase.

That simple ad was the perfect message at the right time in my life. It began a relationship that I maintain to this day with the author of that free report, Eric Ruth, and it eventually led me to a long-standing and prosperous relationship with Dan Kennedy himself. However, it almost didn't happen at all.

I got that free report about three days after leaving my information on that recorded message, but I put it in my read-later pile. Things got busy at work, business was picking up a bit, and I didn't have time to read. But then, while cleaning up my desk at home a few weeks later, I came across the report. It was literally in my hand to toss into the trash. I read the headline one more time, which drew me into the subhead, which drew me into the copy.

I felt like this guy was talking directly to me! My third studio was open, and I had just spent thousands of dollars on an image-driven, completely branded external marketing campaign that hadn't generated one single client. I was fed up and knew that there had to be a better way. So, I sat down on the couch, albeit pessimistically, and read the 22-page free report from cover to cover.

Surprisingly, the report had my undivided attention, and some of the things that I learned in the report I knew could help me. I was eager to begin trying what I later learned to be direct-response marketing. I felt that if there was this much value in the free stuff, there had to be major value in the information for sale.

I called Eric and asked him what he would recommend for me with my three locations and the fourth in development. He asked me tons of questions about my business, our target market, demographics, and everything else he would need to craft a perfect message for my target market. I was a little perturbed by all of the questions and really just wanted him to hand me the magic marketing bullet.

Later I would understand that he was simply working Dan Kennedy's Marketing Triangle (Market, Message, and Media). Once he had all the appropriate information, he promised to build me a campaign and said he would be back in touch soon.

A few weeks later, he sent me a direct-mail marketing campaign that had a three-step letter sequence (which I later learned was classic Kennedy Magnetic Marketing style), with some of the most bizarre instructions I had ever received!

First he wanted me to take a picture of myself literally icing a cake and then paste it on the front of the letter right next to a bizarre headline that said, "I Want to Put the Icing on Your Cake!" Both Aaron and I were immediately indignant and said, "Eric, do you realize I'm sending this to the most influential community in our city? My parents live in that neighborhood. What will they think? I'm not doing it!" He asked me if I was willing to continue to mail my postcards and waste my money. I reluctantly agreed to having my picture taken and pasting it on the letter.

Then he gave specific, seemingly insignificant instructions about what size envelope to use, the type of stamp to apply to the envelope, and the need to get my trainers to hand address each and every letter!

On top of all this, he went on with his instructions for me: when to mail each letter, what day of the week the prospects should receive it, how many days apart each letter should be mailed, and how to create a deadline, an irresistible offer, risk reversal, and a "B" offer with more information that could be requested to help build my list.

I didn't know if this guy was brilliant or a lunatic, but I was desperate for a winning campaign so I followed each and every detail exactly how it was laid out for me. Again, I didn't know I was being introduced to Dan's 10 laws of marketing as found in his *No B.S. Direct Marketing for Non-Direct Marketing Businesses* book.

Once the letters were all created and ready to go, I dropped them in the mailbox and said a quick prayer that I would not become the laughing stock of Birmingham, Alabama! We mailed to a wealthy community called Greystone, containing about 1,000 high-end homes located just outside our newest location.

The results were absolutely amazing. The phone started ringing off the hook! First of all, I couldn't believe the phone was ringing, and secondly, I couldn't believe how presold these prospects were on the program we provided. Because the letter was so well crafted and did the heavy lifting for me, I was having higher quality conversations and then an incredibly high closing rate with much bigger contracts once I got them into my location.

All in all, I ended up generating 41 new one-on-one personal training clients in one month, just from that three-step letter campaign. With an average contract value of more than $2,500.00, this represented the best new business month in my then six-year career in personal training!

I ended up automating the entire campaign through a mailing house, including the live stamp, handwritten addresses, and goofy head-shots. I ran it month-in and month-out in each of my locations. The campaign was so strong that I opened up three more locations that I owned and operated in Birmingham as well as an additional 49 locations that I would develop and oversee throughout the Southeast.

It worked like "gang busters" each and every month. I had a very healthy return on investment (ROI) every month, my business was rocking, and we were opening new locations every six months like clockwork. For almost three years, I literally built my businesses on the backbone of that one three-step letter campaign. Before I ever officially knew the direct-response marketing axiom of selling customers to build a brand instead of trying to build a brand to sell customers, I literally lived it. Every time I hear Dan talk about the value that one single sales letter can have on your business, I know that it's gospel truth!

With my single direct-response letter campaign, I thought I had found the magic bullet. In fact, I'm pretty sure I thought I was bulletproof at that point! Until it stopped working. Painfully, I learned another one of Dan's primary lessons about "the danger of one." One message. One campaign. One media. I only had one bullet in my marketing arsenal.

I had no other campaigns lined up ready to go. I had not been split testing headlines or offers. I had not been developing another campaign to beat the control, so that I could simply roll out the new one when my old one started dropping in returns.

This is really when my journey to understanding direct-response marketing began. I had to know why those stupid letters worked in the first place and then why they, just as mysteriously to me, stopped working. By that point I learned that Eric was studying under some guy named Dan Kennedy, so I started to learn as much as I could about Dan. I subscribed to the *No B.S. Marketing Letter* and read a few of his books. I ended up buying Aaron out of those first three locations. He had been so impressed by his first interaction with direct-response marketing that he went on to become an independent business advisor with GKIC, the company built around Dan Kennedy.

I slowly started to realize that the entire process, from the stamps, to the headline, to the deadlines, were all part of a choreographed process that was only scratching the surface of the options available to me. I dove in deep to "Planet Dan," and started attending some of his events, which eventually led to joining his Platinum and then Titanium Mastermind coaching groups and hiring him for his Private Coaching Group consulting days. But that would be years down the road from this initial experience with Eric.

The Second Bite of the Apple

Out of all this experience came my unique education and new orientation. I wanted to start with a clean slate and build a powerful, meaningful fitness brand fueled by the kind of direct-response marketing that had worked so well. This time, I wanted the best of both worlds; the direct inflow of good customers and fast-rising revenue that direct response had delivered but also the aftereffect of something built to last. I knew I did not want to just be dependent on either one good promotion or one promotion after another.

In late 2009, I was in the process of selling all my existing one-on-one personal training businesses and creating a new group fitness brand from scratch that I intended to franchise from Day One. I knew that I wanted direct-response marketing to be at the core of what we did as a brand, and I resolved that I wouldn't make the same mistake I had before by becoming too reliant on only one campaign or media.

I also knew that I was going to focus on selling customers to build the brand and not try to build the brand to sell customers. That may seem like semantics to some, but I was laser focused on evaluating every marketing action I took with a trackable direct return on investment (D-ROI), and not focusing on the by-product of brand awareness. I hired my former business partner, Aaron, to serve as copywriter and implementor of direct-response marketing. Although we were just a startup business, I knew that this was a position that I couldn't be without.

In short, I was committed to a direct-response marketing effort.

Go to www.IronTribeFranchise.com/NoBS to watch Jim Cavale and Forrest Walden provide commentary on this chapter and see real Iron Tribe marketing samples.

CHAPTER 4

We Build the Brand—By Selling

by Forrest Walden

Now I'm going to show you, step by step, piece by piece, how we raised up our brand by selling memberships.

The new company I was building had started in my garage as an underground "fight club" type workout scene, where you basically had to be one of my close friends to get in. However, when I started to see the amazing results and tight-knit community that this intense, group workout format was generating for my close buddies, I got extremely excited about developing a new concept that I was confident could fill a niche in the industry and become an excellent franchise opportunity.

The only thing I was struggling with was overcoming the "cult" word that kept popping up when people tried to explain what was going on in my little 400-square-foot garage. I knew I had an especially tight community being built, but I really hated the connotation of the word "cult."

The more I played with the concept, the more I realized that what I was building was a "tribe," not a "cult." I knew that the most important asset of a business is its list and that I would have to continue to focus on the community and the exclusivity of belonging to what would be known as "Iron Tribe Fitness."

The next thing that I had to address was the fact that most people simply believed that they couldn't do these intense, group-based workouts. I needed social proof in a hurry, and I also needed a strong "B offer" for all the people that I knew would raise their hands with interest but might be too intimidated to actually walk in and give it a shot.

This led to creating space ads with provocative headlines like "Don't Envy Us, Join Us In The Ultimate Lifestyle Fitness Community," or "If A Picture Is Worth A Thousand Words, Then What Do These Pictures Say About Iron Tribe Fitness?" I came across an old picture of my group at the garage, and I felt like it communicated everything that I was trying to sell, fitness that was fun and effective and being performed with an amazing community of like-minded people. (See Figure 4.1 on page 37.)

That old garage gym picture became our control, because it continued to pull an amazing response every time we ran it. It also led to creating an in-depth free report that was loaded with social proof from people of all walks of life espousing the benefits of the program. The name of the free report was "Why All These Frustrated Men and Women Canceled Their Gym Membership and Started Working Out At Iron Tribe Fitness .

FIGURE 4.1

FIGURE 4.1: continued

> Figure 4.1: **DAN KENNEDY'S COMMENT:** Here is one of those early ads. As you can see, it featured a staple of hard-core direct-response advertising for weight loss or fitness: before and after photos and specific results. More importantly, in the letter from Forrest, it made two offers and a strong guarantee. The Iron Tribe Fitness logo is small, paper-clipped to the little letter (not taking up a third or half the ad space as in most brand-driven ads).

. . And Why <u>You</u> May Want To As Well." We made sure that each and every space ad and advertising medium we used gave the option to request the free report so that we could acquire the prospects' mailing addresses and get this valuable information into their hands as quickly as possible. (See Figure 4.2 on page 39.)

I knew that we needed to create urgency in our marketing message and compel our clients to get started quickly in becoming a part of our new gym community. We decided to focus on premium pricing and the fact that we would have a limit to the number of clients that we could serve (300).

Once that number of memberships was sold, then we would no longer bring on new clients and would place all prospects on a waiting list. We focused on the fact that we were a premium, small, niche, group-training facility and were the complete opposite of the big-box gyms that want to sell as many memberships as possible in hopes that the customers never come!

We were able to leverage this message of scarcity in each and every media that we put our message in and made sure to update the number of memberships sold in each ad, while updating the diminishing number of available memberships left before the waiting list would kick in.

FIGURE 4.2

I couldn't take it anymore, and neither could these guys! Discover...

Why All These Frustrated Men And Women Canceled Their Gym Memberships And Started Working Out At Iron Tribe Fitness ...

Hurry Get Your Hands on this Free Report Now Before It's Too Late.

And Why You May Want To As Well...

From: **Forrest Walden**
Owner, Iron Tribe Fitness

Dear About Town Reader:

We are a lot alike, you and me ...

Like you, I hate wasting my time in a gym. Also like you, if there is a better way to get in the best shape of my life, I want to know about it.

And like many who will read this notice, I spent umpteen years in a "Globo Gym" only getting it half right.

My friends, (pictured above) were getting it half right too. Their one-year transformations have shocked their friends!

How would you enjoy shocking your friends, too?

Hello, my name is **Forrest Walden**, and I'm the owner of **Iron Tribe Fitness** located at 2809 Central Ave. in Homewood. We open our doors to the public on *Monday, February 1st*. We're located down the street from the Homewood park right beside Malcom's Auto.

We specialize in   training.

What can one year of   training at Iron Tribe Fitness do for you? Why don't we find out?

Call me today at **205-874-6300**. But hurry, because we have a **membership cap at only 200 members. Not even 201.**

Interested, but need more information? I can understand that, and that's why I've written a special free report for you entitled ...

"Why All These Frustrated Men And Women Canceled Their Gym Memberships And Started Working Out At **Iron Tribe Fitness ...**
And Why YOU May Want To As Well."

You can get your free copy right now at ...

www.irontribefitness.com/abouttown

I urge you to get your hands on this free report today before the masses who read **About Town** beat you to it, and you end up missing out. Here's the official announcement ...

WANTED:

Only 200, 183, 147, 123 Eager, Determined Birmingham Residents... Both Male and Female ... to Join Our Very Exciting, Very Exclusive Iron Tribe Fitness "Circle of Fitness" Team-Building Program

Fair Warning: You Only Have Until 5:00 PM Friday, February 26th to Get In ... OR ... Until All Membership Slots Are Taken ... Whichever Comes First. The Doors Will Close Quickly ... So Please Hurry ... I Don't Want You To Miss Out!

So call me right now at **874-6300** before the door to this rare invitation slams shut and membership is closed.

Mother of 3 Shocks Her Friends

"I'm a mother of 3 beautiful children, and when I began working out with Iron Tribe Fitness, I didn't have the upper body strength to do a single body-weight chin-up.

But now I can do 25 in a row. My friends are totally shocked! Doing workouts with Iron Tribe Fitness gives me the greatest results I've ever experienced!" - Mendy

2809 CENTRAL AVENUE IN DOWNTOWN HOMEWOOD
Call 874-6300 Now

DAN KENNEDY'S COMMENT: Here's the early ad with the group photo. The emphasis is on the free report offer, but also on the urgency created both by scarcity, with a diminishing number of spots available, and by a specific deadline and the direct offer to call. This is all, again, hard-core direct response. The logo is a little bigger, though.

The response we received was immediate and amazing! We started selling 40 to 50 memberships a month, at double the price of our competitors, and sold our capacity number at that first location in just under eight months! Often the first question that would be asked when we were contacted by a prospect from an ad was whether there were still any spots left from the original 300 available. That is great positioning to begin a sales consultation.

As we developed more and more raving fan testimonials, we started to vary the message and went after different demographics with our ads, such as females and the over-40 crowd. We wanted to continue to dispel the myth that Iron Tribe was only for elite athletes and we weren't for mainstream America.

I started to use my wife as one of my models for the ads. As a busy mother of four, she fit the stay-at-home mom demographic perfectly and really resonated with that demographic. As much as she hated being the star of the ads, they were great for recruiting women who never thought they would be doing our type of intense group workout. (See Figure 4.3 on page 41.)

We were also having success through several different direct-mail campaigns. We did really well at leveraging our own sphere of influence, and eventually we created a three-step direct-mail campaign for new Iron Tribe gyms getting ready to open, and that has done extremely well for us. But we also knew that we would have to create proven external marketing campaigns for our franchisees that were going into new markets, where they didn't have a sphere of influence, so we started to apply much of what I have learned over the years to some very successful postcard, sales letter, and lumpy mail campaigns. One of our most successful direct-mail campaigns is an evergreen

FIGURE 4.3

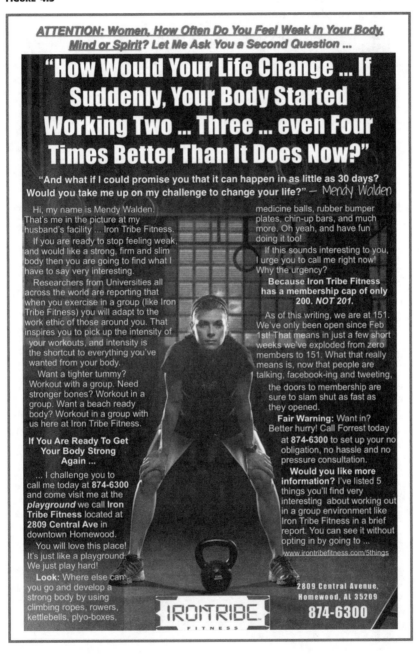

FIGURE 4.3: continued

> Figure 4.3: **DAN KENNEDY'S COMMENT**: Most big-brand advertisers would pale, tremble in fear, and probably criticize this ad as "too tabloid-y," like something you'd see in the *National Enquirer*. They would also think its copy's tone too confrontational and off-putting to many women. About that last point, they would be right. Key word: many. One of the chief principles of great direct-response advertising is that it should repel the wrong customers in order to strongly, magnetically resonate with precisely the right customers, thus always sacrificing many to attract few. This is a great example of using a clear and forceful ad to position a brand-in-the-making.

campaign to neighborhoods around each location. (See Figure 4.4 on page 43.)

We have never wavered in our commitment to selling. A lot of small-business owners and professionals as well as big corporations get weak-kneed about this! During the time this book was being written, a disastrous experiment was run with J.C. Penney in which selling in its advertising was abandoned in favor of vague, feel-good brand messaging. The CEO behind this decision came and went quickly, leaving behind a financially wounded company. We want to build our brand, but we *need* 300 active members enrolled at each of our locations as quickly as possible, so we are patient about our brand-building and act with urgency about our selling.

Go to www.IronTribeFranchise.com/NoBS to watch Jim Cavale and Forrest Walden provide commentary on this chapter and see real Iron Tribe marketing samples.

FIGURE 4.4

The Success of Over 185 of Your Mountain Brook Neighbors Reveal Why You Need To Take A Closer Look At The Only Secret Left On How To Lose Those Last 20 lbs ... And Get In The Best Shape Of Your Life!

Tuesday, 6:35 p.m.

Dear Neighbor,

My name is Forrest Walden, and I'm what some news reporters are calling a "national success story." You may have heard about the nationwide attention I've been receiving in the news over the past few months.

Or you may have seen me on TV, heard me on the radio, or seen articles written about me in *The Wall Street Journal's Market Watch*, *The Birmingham News*, *The Birmingham Business Journal*, and other publications.

But none of that matters right now. What does matter is that I have something urgent to share with you that has the power to change your life forever. It's the only secret left to getting in the best shape of your life. So, What Is This Secret, Exactly?

It's the Secret of Team Workouts ... The Accountability Of Working Side-By-Side Among Teammates <u>Who Care About Your Success</u> ... and <u>Won't Allow You To Quit On Yourself!</u> That's because working together as a team changes the rules of fitness and turns the whole concept on its head, and when applied scientifically and skillfully (as Teresa discovered ... and you will too!), it is a real life changer. And you'll have **more fun working out than ever**, because Iron Tribe is literally the sport of fitness.

Picture a room full of individuals all doing the same workout at the same time, and everyone in the class is encouraging everyone else to finish the workout. It's a workout for all ages and both sexes, and when done right delivers unparalleled fitness results. Iron Tribe Fitness offers varied, purposeful and truly fun workouts.

There's nothing like it anywhere to get you into the best shape of your life. You will possess an amazingly athletic body with extraordinary strength and your body control will amaze your friends. As Teresa (and hundreds more of your neighbors) can attest, it's the Iron Tribe EXPERIENCE that's REALLY the best part. Teresa goes on to brag about the team community of Iron Tribe Fitness:

You're invited to stop by our location on 15 Dexter Avenue, not far from where you live, to claim your $145 Fitness Gear-Bag and meet the staff and other Iron Tribe Fitness members... We are looking for a few new members. Our facilities are designed for ONLY 250 members ... NOT 2,000 and we are filling up fast!

...So come in, let us give you a free fitness consultation and evaluation, collect your $145 Gear-Bag and see if we fit in with your fitness and health goals. All you have to do is say, "maybe" right now by contacting us or stopping in. We realize you may still be skeptical - that's why we want you to stop in and check us out – no obligations....GUARANTEED.

You're Protected By My Iron Clad, 100% Money Back Guarantee

There Are No Strings Attached

No Fine Print, and No Obligations.

It Doesn't Matter Your Age, Gender or Current Fitness Level, Either.

What Does Matter Is, You Will Discover The Only Secret Left To Getting In The Best Shape Of Your Life ... And Why I'm Ethically Bribing You With A Special Fitness Packet To Get You Started.

$145.00 VALUE

"I actually look forward to pushing myself and supporting my fellow "tribers" each week. You are held accountable every workout. You feel a close bond with your teammates, and we all help each other along in our daily struggles. I began to feel that I belonged to a community. I began to feel that the Tribe was my team and my family."

BEFORE   AFTER   254

FIGURE 4.4: continued

 Figure 4.4: **DAN KENNEDY'S COMMENT**: This is an oversized (8½" x 11") two-sided postcard, with a classic "bribe offer" (Free Fitness Gear Bag) and a free try-before-you-buy offer (Free Fitness Consultation). Notice how little space is given to Iron Tribe branding—in fact, find the logo if you can! This is all about getting prospects to sales appointments where memberships can be sold. It actually takes a lot of courage NOT to plaster one's brand logo, image, and slogans all over everything. A lot of Forrest's and Jim's brand development is from the Tribe out, rather than by sacrificing selling to outright advertise it to the world. This is actually how Apple built its brand early on, but few remember now that it is so iconic.

CHAPTER 5

Criticism Will Come; Thick Skin Is Required

by Forrest Walden

e were having a great time creating and running all of the different campaigns that we were building. They were returning anywhere from 200% to 400% ROI a month, and we were thrilled.

However, there was a small problem. My wife hated the ads, and our clients kept telling me that the advertising didn't reflect the quality of the program and the quality of the brand. I was told our advertising was "unprofessional." I had many heated conversations with my graphic designer, who helped me develop the mark and logo, about how bad the advertisements I was running were. Everyone (including our investor) was telling us that nobody would ever read the 30-page free report that we were mailing out and that we were wasting so much money using snail mail.

I'll never forget talking to a surgeon, who was an absolute raving fan of our service, and hearing him tell me that he wasn't proud of our brand when he saw the advertising. I was deeply troubled. As I asked him more and more questions, I realized that he had actually come from one of those very same ads, requested a free report, and read it cover to cover. As Dan Kennedy says, "Buyers are liars!"

Our advertising was "crushing it," and we started opening more and more locations in Birmingham, using the same campaigns and adding even more urgency, leveraging the fact that we had literally sold out two locations and had waiting lists.

We knew that we had to have more than a prototype to show that we had successfully replicated our model and that we needed to establish a true system that was ready to franchise.

When we opened our third location and started finalizing the franchise process, we started to realize that we had a raving fan base and a true brand that was being built. However, we also knew that when franchisees look to purchase the franchise, they were going to want some strong branding campaigns as well as the "tried and true" direct-response campaigns that we had been building and testing so effectively.

I remembered the story from Dan's *Renegade Millionaire* audio CDs, where the CEO from Weight Watchers said that Dan's stuff out-pulled his advertising agency's work easily, but he could never use it because it was too ugly and his board as well as the franchisees would turn it down.

We needed to start creating some campaigns that not only had direct-response elements, but also could leverage our rapidly growing brand. Unfortunately, we thought we had to go out and find an advertising agency to help us pull that off.

I am describing an evolution and maturation of a business's identity and brand, and of its relationship with its tribe, that is very sensitive and hazardous. Giving your tribe what it wants and needs to feel proud and eager to recruit customers for you and making your brand more recognizeable as a brand while staying true to the marketing principles, strategies, and tactics that got the business to success and that are required to fuel its sales is like being a blind tightrope walker on a windy day. It's easy to stumble here, and we did. And we learned from our mistakes.

One thing is very important: Critics will assemble around you and may get more vocal the more successful and visibly successful you become. I believe you have to listen to all voices—but unemotionally. You have to listen most to your actual customers' voices. Ultimately, though, you must listen to your own voice.

Go to www.IronTribeFranchise.com/NoBS to watch Jim Cavale and Forrest Walden provide commentary on this chapter and see real Iron Tribe marketing samples.

CHAPTER 6

Adventures with Ad Agencies

by Jim Cavale

W e all have an incident that we can recall as kids, where we were warned not to touch something, but yet as soon as we had the chance, we went and touched exactly what mom and dad said not to!

You only have to read Dan Kennedy's *No B.S. Direct Marketing For Non-Direct Marketing Businesses* one time to know that ad agencies don't really understand direct-response marketing nor do they want to. The warning is clear.

I remember bringing up the option of bringing in a Chief Marketing Officer (CMO) or hiring an advertising agency at one of my Platinum Mastermind hot seat sessions, and Dan summed it up by saying, "Don't bite the hand that has fed you." That's not the only time he has told us that we should never stop developing and overseeing the direct-response marketing strategies, since that is the basis for our success in the first place.

Yet for some reason, Forrest and I still felt led to begin pursuing and interviewing advertising agencies, with aspirations for relief from our marketing duties so that we could focus heavily on all of the "more important stuff" that's required to actually go out and franchise your brand. There's a lot of operational work, like following the Federal Trade Commission's (FTC) requirements for all new franchisor brands, such as creating our Franchise Disclosure Documents (FDD) and operations manual tools, let alone stepping up all of our systems and opening up more corporately owned gyms in the Birmingham market.

Those things are vital, especially during the creation phase. But I am here to tell you that none of it matters if you lose control of your marketing, and essentially your brand. Which is exactly what we did when we tested out working with an ad agency early on.

First, we set out on a six-month tour of multiple agencies who pitched our up-and-coming brand on how they could be the marketing solution for our expansion in Birmingham and beyond. It was quite interesting listening to the diverse feedback we were getting on what we had done to that point and how these potential ad agency partners felt like they could take it and not only improve it, but also scale it to multiple markets. It is flattering to be told good things about your brand, but also intimidating and troubling to hear a lot of criticism about how you are presenting that brand.

We heard it all. From questions about the "nonexistent graphic design and layout" that they thought we desperately needed to improve, to concerns about "the amount of excessive copy that we had in our print ads and email templates."

There were even pitches that were self-eliminating, as several agencies felt like they didn't want to step in and "mess up" what we had already established, even though they didn't really understand why it worked.

Either way, the search took six months because it was highly underwhelming. It felt wrong, but we still chose to give it the ole' college try and test it out by choosing an agency that we assumed could actually learn our direct-response style and then help us continue to scale it.

As we ran our test, we realized that Dan was exactly right; we couldn't ever expect a marketing agency to understand our style of marketing enough to be able to improve upon it in an innovative way that could grow our brand into new markets. WE HAD TO DO IT OURSELVES.

They didn't embrace us, nor did they even read the Dan Kennedy tools that we put in their hands with hopes they'd become junkies just like us. However, like all tests, we learned a great deal from it, and honestly, it further emphasized the fact that we could indeed begin to combine the direct-response and branding strategies into a powerful hybrid far more valuable than either extreme could ever service on its own.

DAN KENNEDY'S COMMENT: There are three vital points made here by Jim that I want to be absolutely certain aren't missed. First, I resolutely teach there are two things never, never, never to give up control over in your business: the checkbook and the marketing. It is infinitely easier to replace yourself in technical and operational roles than in the driver's seat of your advertising and marketing. Whether you keep that a

DAN KENNEDY'S COMMENT, continued

do-it-yourself effort, with a few in-house staffers or a few outside freelancers, or you manage to pull off the feat they didn't and find an outside agency that understands or is willing to understand the unusual hybrid of direct response and brand taught in this book, you must never abdicate authority. I was taught early in my business life a simple truth: Two people cannot ride side by side on the same horse. There can only be one person with the reins. That has to be you. That does not mean you want obsequious yes-men and yes-women merely doing your bidding. It does mean when you do consider ideas and input and arrive at your vision, your leadership decisions, and your tactical plan for your marketing, your team makes it their business to understand it, embrace it, and implement it.

Second, when you turn to outsiders for assistance with advertising and marketing, make evidence of their understanding of, respect for, and preferably successful experience with direct-response marketing a requirement. The advertising and marketing world's population of idea-rich theorists and outright nincompoops has expanded wildly in recent years as online media has brought forward an array of *technicians* (web designers, social media managers, blog writers, etc.) who grab the reins of marketing yet have no successful marketing or selling experience. Beware them. A bricklayer is not an architect.

Third, last, do not underestimate yourself or undervalue your own knowledge of your business. Just because someone has a trophy case of ad industry awards (from peers—not based on clients' profits), or two Ph.D.s from big-name universities, or big-name corporations as clients does not mean his judgment

---

DAN KENNEDY'S COMMENT, continued

is superior to yours about your brand, your customers, and your marketing. You don't want to be arrogant or close-minded, but you can't let yourself be intimidated or unduly influenced either. I have two key questions I like to use, that you might appropriate, when there is an expert or a critic confronting me: 1) why do you believe I should think differently about this? and 2) what *facts* do you have to support your position? Facts are important, and much harder to come by than opinions or criticism. I am willing to be persuaded by facts. In a toss-up on competing, conflicting opinions about my business, I'll take mine.

Go to www.IronTribeFranchise.com/NoBS to watch Jim Cavale and Forrest Walden provide commentary on this chapter and see real Iron Tribe marketing samples from our test with an ad agency!

CHAPTER 7

Our Winning Formula:

Get Clients with Direct Response, Keep Clients Engaged, Proud, and Evangelistic with Brand

by Jim Cavale

Our nine-month tug-of-war test with a local ad agency taught Forrest and me a great deal about marketing in general. We always thought it was ironic that the same direct-response marketing style that brings in new clients is the marketing that they complain to us about months later.

The facts are the facts in the respect that we have created a client experience that recruits Iron Tribe member athletes to feel some serious ownership of the brand. It's pretty intense, just like our workouts!

The surgeon that Forrest made note of earlier is just one of dozens of examples that we had to have thick skin in dealing with. It caused us to wonder if it might just be worth creating brand-centric marketing that our clients can take pride in, even if it wouldn't initially return as well as the pure direct-response stuff.

I said "initially return" because the average Iron Tribe member athlete does indeed refer 1.3 people to join their tribe and renews their membership agreement at least one time, which means if brand-centric marketing helps our athletes take more pride in the Iron Tribe membership, it could eventually be tied to an actual ROI.

Another way to think about this, which we've discussed at length with Dan, is that there is front-end ROI and back-end ROI. Front end and back end are direct-marketing industry terms that people in other fields may not be familiar with. Simply put, front end is everything leading up to and including the first transaction, when someone first becomes a client. Back end is everything that happens afterward, in the ongoing relationship with and monetization of that client. Front-end ROI has to do with the cost of getting customers through advertising and marketing and the return on those invested dollars from that first transaction or a series of transactions occurring one right after the other in the short term. Back-end ROI is more complicated. It has to factor in retention and longevity, frequency of purchase, continuity or renewal income, ascension, and, very important but often not managed or measured or accounted for, referral activity.

We began thinking about our most aggressive direct-response advertising and marketing as front end, and by the way, a front-end necessity, and about a need for more motivational, brand-oriented messaging as back end.

Forrest and I agreed that if we were going to start testing out these strategies at our own gyms in Birmingham, we had to be able to track it enough to justify it. The preceding statistics of average member athlete referrals and renewal rates would be our barometer for success, with a goal of maintaining an average of more than one referral and membership agreement renewal per member athlete, but ideally seeing improvement.

We also knew that to pull this test off, we would have to invest into an implementation team that would be based in our corporate offices, since we felt continuing with our ad agency was not worth the offset in our marketing budget.

Daniel Walters, an Iron Tribe member athlete who had lost more than 100 pounds and was already working in the tech and digital marketing world at another firm in Birmingham, would become the first member of our "marketing implementation team." As our Marketing Implementer, Daniel's objective is to carry out not only our already-in-play direct-response marketing load but also new initiatives like this brand-marketing centric test.

We started with a different look, feel, and overall format in our *TribeVibe* newsletter, which became much more "pretty" and features the faces of our member athletes on its cover. We now use the inside content areas to review and preview local Iron Tribe events in each respective market, along with providing fitness and nutrition resources featuring our top coaches as the experts providing these tools to enrich the member athlete experience. (See Figures 7.1A through D starting on page 58.)

Our decision to invest in an implementation team immediately expanded our in-house capabilities, not just with a slicker monthly newsletter design and strategy but also in establishing the ability to scale it in a graphically designed, templated format for each newly franchised market to utilize as a communication tool with their tribe.

The next idea within this experiment was to leverage my on-camera broadcasting capabilities that I had honed in college and even professionally while working for networks

FIGURE 7.1A: Iron Tribe Newsletter

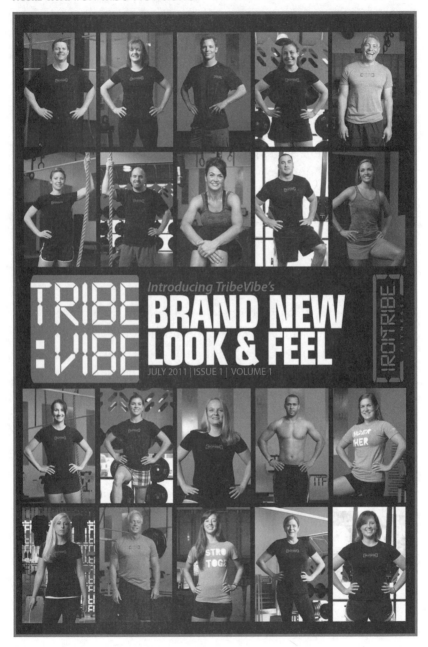

FIGURE 7.1B: Iron Tribe Local Event in Newsletter

Figures 7.1A–D: **DAN KENNEDY'S COMMENT**: Forrest and Jim wisely began carefully and gradually transitioning their marketing to and through their members to a more brand-driven, graphic approach. The newsletter's facelift made it more of a professional-looking magazine. What they understood, that many businesspeople don't, is that you can and should present yourself differently to different audiences at different times. And while front-end marketing has to heavily rely on specific promises and claims, promotional offers, and urgency for immediate response, back-end marketing can revolve more around social proof, human interest, and demonstration of community. It is difficult to reverse that and put sense of community and prideful belonging out there as the front-end, absent

FIGURE 7.1C: Iron Tribe *TribeVibe* Letter

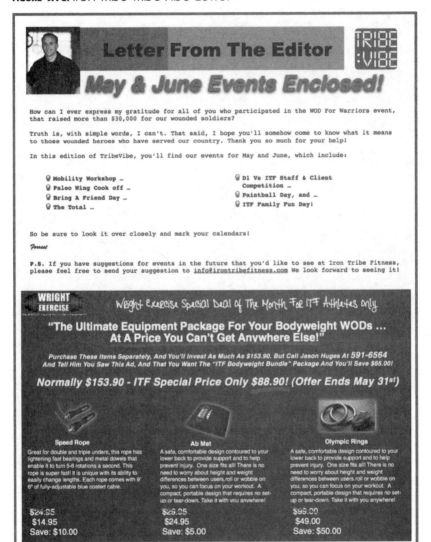

FIGURE 7.1D: Iron Tribe *TribeVibe* Letter

Figures 7.1A–D: **DAN KENNEDY'S COMMENT**, continued

promises, offers, and urgency. Companies that try it or insist on it waste a great deal of money that can't be held accurately accountable for ROI, and can even go broke creating a well-known brand that is favorably thought of but doesn't sell anything!

The winning formula Jim describes here is a great way to balance direct-response and brand in a business.

---

like ESPN. This led to what is now known as *TribeVibeTV*, a weekly show that airs on our YouTube channel and is filtered into each gym's respective website, social media channels, and our iPhone app.

To assist Daniel with this, we brought on a full-time Creative Implementer position to handle both the graphic design needs for offline media layouts and to fulfill the weekly videography that would be required to execute this new *TribeVibeTV* initiative. (See Figures 7.2A–B below and on page 63.)

If we learned anything from Dan Kennedy's *Renegade Millionaire* audio CDs, it is the fact that you can never spend enough marketing dollars, nor can you ever be present in

FIGURE 7.2A: Iron Tribe *TribeVibe TV*

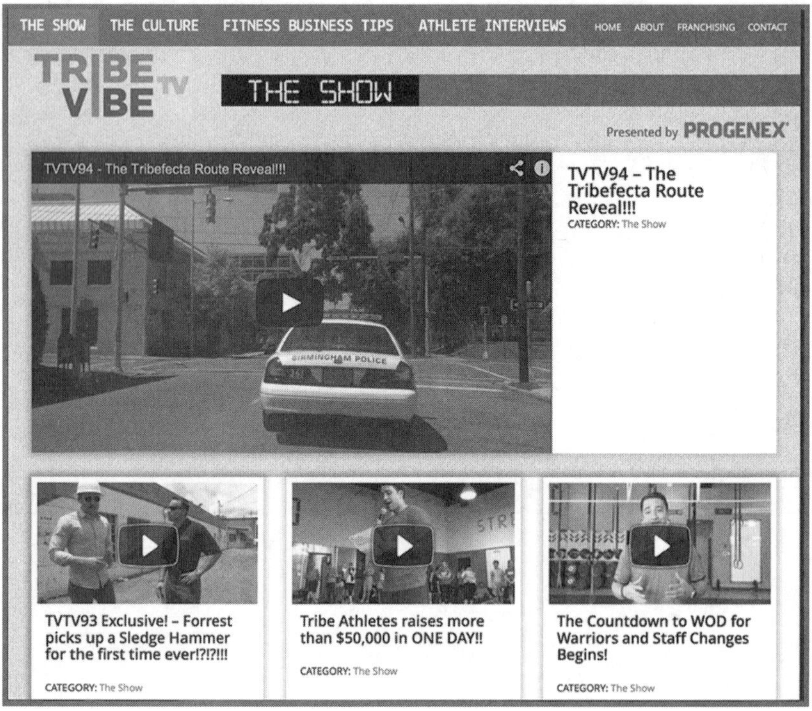

FIGURE 7.2B: Iron Tribe *TribeVibe TV*

> Figures 7.2A–B: **DAN KENNEDY'S COMMENT**: Notice the view
> counts for the different segments of *TribeVibeTV*. Do they seem
> small to you? Direct-response marketing is much about *target* marketing.
> Giant audience is rarely the goal. What's important to a company like Iron
> Tribe is not how many know it and engage with it, but that the right clients
> and prospective clients know it and engage with it. This is a great hybrid
> of direct-response messages integrated with brand identity for members
> and those they tell about and refer to their tribe. It's also worth noting that
> Iron Tribe has a second audience to consider and appeal to: new franchise
> owners, many of whom rise up from their members. Just about every
> communication effort they invest in, including this one, needs to reinforce
> the idea that theirs is not only a life-altering fitness phenomenon but also a
> business success phenomenon. You can see current *TribeVibeTV* at www.
> tribevibetv.com or youtube.com/TribeVibeTV.

enough places. One of my favorite stories is of the business
owner who bought billboard space near his competitor's home,
knowing that it wasn't necessarily in an area that could generate
new leads but that it would simply discourage his competitor.

This is the perception we want to create for Iron Tribe, within each respective market where our brand has its gyms being developed: that we are everywhere. That we are powerful. The reason I have coined it as "YOUbiquity" is because when it's fully achieved, YOU truly cannot get rid of us even if you try. We're everywhere!

The unique advantage with our "YOUbiquitous" journey is the fact that we have an extra media that most don't—the voices of our member athletes. They are true evangelists for their tribe, fighting for us right now on the streets as you read this very chapter.

For instance, you might hear an Iron Tribe direct-response radio commercial and turn the station, only to see us on a billboard en route to your home, just before picking up a print publication with one of our direct-response ads and throwing it aside. And right when you think you've gotten rid of us, your colleague at work says, "Have I told you about this Iron Tribe thing that I'm doing? It's amazing!"—and he directs you to *TribeVibeTV* and gives you a copy of the *TribeVibe* magazine.

This is "YOUbiquity," and I feel like I could write a whole 'nother book on it.

Having six of our own Iron Tribe gyms in a medium-sized market like Birmingham (1.2 million people in the metro area) has not only taught us the power of "YOUbiquity," but also it's held us accountable to the fiduciary responsibility to multiply what was one marketing budget at one gym into as many budgets as there are gyms in that respective market.

This, of course, is one of several advantages when it comes to franchising—economies of scale.

For example, if you have $4,000.00 allotted to invest into your Iron Tribe gym's marketing each month and you stick to our proven development schedule of opening a new gym every nine months, you are consistently adding to your monthly marketing spend each year, from $4,000.00 per month, to $8,000.00 per month, to where we are today, at $24,000.00 per month.

Our three-year journey in Birmingham, from one gym to six, became the gauge by which we began to make decisions with this budget on direct-response-style advertising versus brand-centric.

Because of this, we've been able to create a system for all of our franchisees to follow, mapping out this investment strategy starting 60 days before they even open their doors, which of course is going to be a pure direct-response strategy, going back to Forrest's chapter on "We Build the Brand—By Selling."

However, as Iron Tribe franchise owners begin to fill up their first gym with member athletes, there are brand-centric marketing pieces that they're prompted to invest time and money into, encouraging retention and referrals amongst their initial member athlete base.

Cutting-edge technology development is a big part of this as well. It's one thing to put your message out there in public medias like print, SEO, SEM, billboards, direct mail, TV, and radio (we use all of these), but when you can actually create your own medias that are only filled with your message geared just for your clients, you're tapping into an exclusivity factor that they will appreciate AND you've established a proprietary channel where only you can market to them. Dan Kennedy says that virtually every business—even something as seemingly ordinary as a Main Street shoe store—should be in the media business, too, and own their own media.

Don't Sell to Customers—Totally Involve Customers

We've made it so that downloading the Iron Tribe iPhone app and becoming a member of an Iron Tribe gym's website are absolute non-negotiables. It's a staple in the Iron Tribe experience, where members must go EVERY DAY (or night) to schedule themselves for one of the classes at any of the Iron Tribe gyms in their local market, along with finding out what tomorrow's workout is, which is like a game to them.

They simply cannot go to sleep without knowing what tomorrow will hold, and they don't find out until about 7:30 s ℙ . each evening, when the next day's workout is finally announced. It's like the NCAA March Madness Selection Show, but every night!

Analytics on their personal progression toward their goals, account information on food and product purchases, and a constant stream of microblog communication from other tribe athletes and coaches are just a few of the strong engagement aspects that take the Iron Tribe experience beyond the 45-minute class and four walls of the gym.

If the competitive style of our workout programming has created an addictive game, the technology aspect has taken that game and created a league where these games take place. Thus, it is a forum for us to market upcoming events, new products, contract-renewal upgrades, and ultimately, the ability to communicate with members on a regular basis. (See Figures 7.3A–C starting on page 67.)

Through these brand-building strategies, we know that Iron Tribe is more than just our faces as the leaders of the business. We've earned the logo some serious legitimacy, starting with selling memberships via direct-response marketing in each new market and then leveraging things like our monthly *TribeVibe* newsletter, weekly *TribeVibeTV* show, and addictive technology that has become a private media just for us to channel our marketing through, with each client subscribing to it religiously.

FIGURE 7.3A: Iron Tribe Client U

FIGURE 7.3B: Iron Tribe Dashboard

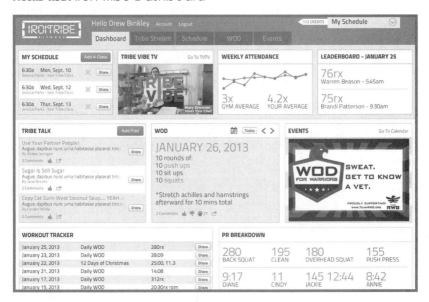

FIGURE 7.3C: Iron Tribe Tribe Stream

Figures 7.3A–C: **DAN KENNEDY'S COMMENT:** Iron Tribe's "client's site" is a sophisticated piece of media. Positioned as the dashboard the member uses on a day-to-day basis to manage his experience and achievement, it literally compels constant engagement. This is not, candidly, easy to figure out for every business, but it is well worth working hard to figure out! This is also outstanding brand reinforcement, with brand advertising appearing throughout. But it also, as Jim points out, gives Iron Tribe the equivalent of its own daily newspaper read religiously by its members, in which it can insert direct-response advertising for events, products, and services. Their ownership of their own media is powerful, but the fact that it draws attention every day is even more powerful.

Go to www.IronTribeFranchise.com/NoBS to watch Jim Cavale and Forrest Walden provide commentary on this chapter and see real Iron Tribe marketing samples.

CHAPTER 8

Skating on Thin Ice:

Advancing Brand, from Back End to Front End

by Jim Cavale

As I described, we evolved to a winning formula, with direct response dominating our front-end or external marketing to the world at large and brand dominating our back-end or internal marketing to and through our members. It worked. But we were involved in a business's evolutionary process, not an arrival at a fixed destination.

We established direct response to sell athlete memberships at each gym, building a growing number of tribes that each athlete member felt an allegiance to. This then allowed for the brand-centric marketing strategies to encourage them to feel prideful association with a brand that is much bigger than just themselves.

But one thing that we began to ask ourselves was how we could better leverage the brand that we've built, while still putting solid lead-generating direct-response marketing out there.

This is not easy.

The ad agency experiment (and my passion for the TV hit series *Mad Men*) had spurred ideas in my head of infusing a traditional brand-building strategy with direct-response fundamentals. However, it has not necessarily been an instant success, but it's definitely been a valuable learning experience. But that's the advantage of having your own corporate gyms to use as innovation test kitchens.

Our system is based on a "do as we do" foundation and NOT just telling our franchise partners to "do as we say." It's always frustrated Forrest and me to watch the consultants out there coaching people to do things they've never even had experience in, telling them to spend the money and time required without knowing whether that advice is going to work.

This next experiment started with a basic idea. I told myself that if Iron Tribe was going to be a household brand name, then I needed to make sure that we had our very own marketing tagline that our member athletes can cling to (i.e., Nike's "Just Do It"), as well as a tagline that could be the source for all our social proof that would continue to be embedded within ALL types of marketing messages.

Dan Kennedy often talks about the breakthrough power of identifying and communicating what business you are really in and urges people to separate their deliverables from that real business.

When we looked at the testimonial emails that clients constantly sent our way on a daily basis, a consistent theme emerged that moves Iron Tribe way beyond just fitness into the most powerful thing that any business could sell: TRANSFORMATION.

Observing the most powerful brands out there, they've taken a commodity, good, or service, and translated it into a superior customer experience. Starbucks personifies this in their ability to take a four-cent cup o' coffee and charge $4.00 for it. Their "third place atmosphere" (in addition to home and work) has generated an experience that customers simply have to have. In Kennedy Language, their coffee is just a deliverable. Their real business is providing that third place. In the evolution of our brand and our marketing, we decided that the gyms, the classes, the workouts, even the media were all deliverables. The real business we were in was transformation.

If you put this book down right now, travel to your closest Iron Tribe, and start talking to member athletes, I am confident you'll consistently hear about their personal transformations, which have gone far beyond the physical fitness results they signed up for in the first place.

Instead, these transformations are filled with feel-good stories about improved marriages, fatherhoods, friendships, careers, and so many other tales of what I tagged as "LIFE. Changed."

At Iron Tribe, we are continuously transforming lives, and the social proof of this lies inside these real stories of "LIFE. Changed." that our direct-response formula has continuously leveraged to generate leads. Meanwhile, our brand-based marketing utilizes this social proof to build the allegiance that each member athlete has toward the Iron Tribe logo.

Don't get confused. The experiments of incorporating "LIFE. Changed." into our direct-response lead-generation marketing has not so much increased external prospect response as much as it's "puffed up the chests" of our internal member athletes. It's cost us time and money, with months of lower ROI success at the beginning, but in the end it's expedited our brand-building aspirations.

We have learned several ways to cage this brand-centric marketing beast, which can truly be a blessing and a curse.

First, we tell our franchise owners that it's only something to roll out after they've reached membership capacity at a minimum of one of the Iron Tribe gyms in their market, since they'll have no member athletes to highlight or make proud of the advertising when they first open up.

You HAVE to HAVE clients before you ever think of marketing the brand. Earn your logo some respect! This applies, in my mind, to any and every business. It can be quick, but there is a sequential process required before you get to full-on, simultaneous use of brand with direct-response everywhere, all the time. If you are already there but struggling, you may need to stop, back up, go back to the beginning, and restart your business just as we started the first Iron Tribe and still start each new geographic area.

Second, you have to be willing to allot the cost of this message as something that will just pay for itself (i.e., at least a 100% ROI) versus a direct-response message that could return as much as 300%. You're not doing it to directly build membership, but more as an initiative that will maintain it. However, when you revisit the stat of 1.3 referrals and more than one contract renewal per member athlete, it's safe to tell yourself that this test has been an overall success. Similar benchmark statistics or numbers are needed in your business.

Change your goals a bit, and understand that while your black-and-white objective ROI goals are still important, you also need to gauge the subjective feelings of your clientele with these brand-centric campaigns. Having conversations with them and even running surveys are ways to quantify this aspect a bit further.

The neatest part of the campaign is the systematized capability to customize it to each respective member athlete's story in a way each can have their very own "LIFE. Changed." tale that lives not only in external advertising but also in our segmented prospect mail and email nurturing sequences. And, of course, these stories now have their own section in our online medias on the iPhone app and website.

One of my favorite stories is of a female member athlete named Erin, who came into our second-ever Iron Tribe gym as a cancer patient looking for more energy and confidence while deep in her battle with chemotherapy. During her initial year of athlete membership at Iron Tribe, Erin's attitude was fearless in her eventual victory over cancer, which she tells in her "LIFE. Changed." story entitled "LIFE. Conquered." Each story has a customized "LIFE. Changed." sub-tagline word, describing each personal transformation. (See Figure 8.1 on page 74.)

This has become a powerful testimonial portal that can be leveraged in all forms of online and offline media.

We've even built a customized prospect segmenting system that allows us to customize the types of mail and email content prospects receive, including which "LIFE. Changed." stories they can read, watch, and connect to our brand even more because of the personal alignment they'll feel with the story they're reading. You can see it online at *www. IronTribeFranchise.com/NoBS*.

Externally, we've began to tell these stories of "LIFE. Changed." in print and digital SEM medias, amongst others, and then utilize detailed calls to action allowing people to continue on to a specific URL where they can watch Erin tell an expanded version of her story. This allows us to track response and conversion, ensuring that this branded campaign still has direct-response quantification fundamentals embedded inside its DNA.

FIGURE 8.1: Iron Tribe "LIFE. Changed." Ad

FIGURE 8.1: Iron Tribe "LIFE. Changed." Ad, continued

> Figure 8.1: **DAN KENNEDY'S COMMENT:** This approach worked out by Jim for Iron Tribe is frankly fraught with peril but is just about the best you could do when merging and integrating and cross-breeding direct response with a brand message in external, public advertising. Breeding these two advertising disciplines is like porcupines breeding—they do it very carefully. You will see that they have removed the hard-core A or B direct-response offer (i.e., call for appointment now or download or ask for this free report now) with a softer, less urgent invitation to go see the testimonial's story online—and there they return to specific offers. Candidly, this makes me nervous. But I congratulate them on stopping short of too far, of too much sacrifice. Just do not miss Jim's point that this has to occur at the right time in a business's development. It is essentially a luxury affordable only at a certain level of sales and profits.

While the lead-generation results of "LIFE. Changed." are not as high as the pure direct-response content that we continue to pump out externally at an average of 300% or better, the pride factor established amongst our clients has been priceless.

A Different Kind of Lead Generation

Lead generation or prospect attraction by paid advertising is one thing, and has its own measurements and ROI. But there's rarely a better customer than a referred customer. By accepting less impressive ROI from this brand-oriented campaign than other direct-response campaigns, we invested in a different kind of lead generation: referrals.

The pride factor became a referral tool that has taken our already sky-high referral rate to another level. It was actually a product of conversation on a private client day with Dan Kennedy, where we all had a realization that even though our clients are evangelists, they don't really have a bible or tracts to hand out to their friends that they want to recruit to their local tribe.

Think about it. We do these high-intensity workouts and charge an average of more than $250.00 per month for membership in this tribe. So our clients' average descriptions end up unintentionally sounding something like "Hey, you need to really consider joining Iron Tribe, where the workouts are so extremely difficult that I'm always sore, and it costs about $300.00 per month."

Not such a good elevator pitch!

However, when we started putting the "LIFE. Changed." stories in their hands, it eased the effort of getting their friends to come to one of our Bring-A-Friend Day events, where they can do a partner workout with their friend, and then sign 'em up to join the tribe.

The private client meeting led us to provide our member athletes with better tools for referrals and better training for them to do so. Dan also made sure he emphasized the fact that we should "reward them for the behavior," meaning that whether or not the referral they give us actually converts into a new member athlete, the referrer should be rewarded for trying in the first place.

And reward them with something outside of the brand, not free product or membership. This led us to providing referrers with VIP experiences such as dinners at the finest restaurants in town and gear from their favorite clothing brands.

The idea of equipping and training our member athletes to refer actually led to an entire box, engineered with an Apple-like look and feel and composed of "LIFE. Changed."

resources for them to give to their friends, free sample nutritional products for them to taste, free merchandise for them to wear in their workouts, a protein shaker bottle, bumper stickers, and a even a blank slate for them to begin writing their "LIFE. Changed." story as well.

Of course, all of these things are branded with our colors, logos, and overall look, knowing that we are literally teaching our clients from Day One to help us grow the tribe.

You can watch a video simulation of receiving an Iron Tribe welcome kit by visiting www.IronTribeFranchise. com/NoBS.

Dan likes to refer to these strategies, and the referral results that come with them, as having created a "cult following." But as Forrest mentioned earlier, we prefer to use the word "tribe," as it fits so perfectly within the context of our name and what we really are.

Just recently, the ultimate branding validation occurred when one of our franchisees had the Iron Tribe logo tattooed on his shoulder. (See Figure 8.2 on page 78.)

When we saw his picture posted and spread all over Facebook, I looked at Forrest and said, "I think it's safe to say that this branding ROI is the equivalent to our 300% direct-response ROI!"

Go to www.IronTribeFranchise.com/NoBS to watch Jim Cavale and Forrest Walden provide commentary on this chapter and see real Iron Tribe marketing samples as well as a special presentation of their referral-generating welcome kit.

FIGURE 8.2: Iron Tribe Logo Tattoo

CHAPTER 9

A Powerful Brand
Needs the Power
to Implement

by Jim Cavale

great brand is built, sustained, and supported by communication, marketing, and direct-response marketing. That's the most fundamental premise of Iron Tribe. We have to be able to communicate our brand massage to our members and to the world in ways that can be efficiently managed and accurately tracked and evaluated for ROI.

We were at our first ever *GKIC SuperConference* in Chicago (2011), when Forrest and I heard about this CRM (Customer Relationship Management) software called Infusionsoft. Already frustrated with our CRM system and the client scheduling and billings software we were using to run our then two gyms, we knew we needed a technological solution that was more congruent with the high-level client experience we were planning to scale.

Our desire was to build an entire platform that I named *The Bay Door* (since we have a signature roll-up bay door in just about every Iron Tribe gym), which I was hoping to provide each franchisee as a "soup-to-nuts" platform with two user interfaces (UI). The vision was for one set of client UI's (website, in-store iPad app for product purchasing, and an iPhone app) and one UI for staff (to run their Iron Tribe gym in all capacities). The goal was to automate as many activities as possible while making anything done manually much easier.

My previous business was a 2008 tech startup where I was constantly overseeing developers, and I had learned enough to know that you can build anything you want—if you have detailed specifications mapped out, lots of cash, and some serious patience. However, without these things, you're in for a run you may not be able to sustain or outlast. Many have tried. Most have failed.

As we "spec'd out" the project, several development firms were quoting the project to cost as much as seven figures! There wasn't one firm who thought the project would cost less than six figures.

However, there was a group of Iron Tribe member athletes who saw the same potential that I did, and we came together to produce something pretty special for a brand as young as ours, for a much lower front-end investment with invaluable back-end prosperity opportunities for everyone involved.

The big idea for *The Bay Door* was simple. Create an Iron Tribe-specific Application Program Interface (API) hub that could leverage pre-built intranet (Google Apps and Yammer) and CRM (Infusionsoft) technologies to integrate with a custom-built client experience engine.

All that means is that cloud-based "software as a service" (SaaS) platforms like Google Apps, Yammer, and Infusionsoft have created API plug-ins that allow you to "pipe it in" to your own custom software and essentially leverage their functionalities to look and feel like your brand.

As simple as it sounds, it can become very complex. As this build began, I also began to test and integrate Infusionsoft into our then two gyms. The process of integrating it into those gyms was an amazing education process for Forrest and me. It forced us to look at the entire sales, marketing, and operations life cycle that each client experiences on the front end, and then systematize it in a way for our staff to monitor and act on in the back end, unless that action can be automated, in which case you just DO NOTHING!

I coined the sales, marketing, and operations life cycle as *The Perfect Athlete Life Cycle,* and to this day, we are continuing to develop it more and more with automated and manual, external and internal marketing strategies. (See Figures 9.1A and B.)

FIGURE 9.1A: Iron Tribe Fitness Client Management

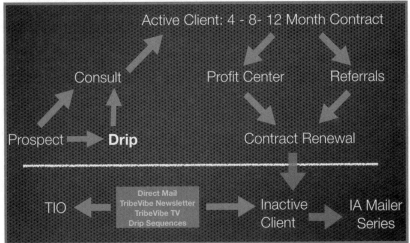

FIGURE 9.1B: Iron Tribe Perfect Athlete Life Cycle

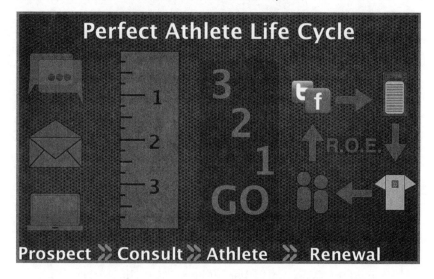

While our developers began working away at the first version of *The Bay Door* technology, our Infusionsoft experiment was bearing a great deal of fruit. Our gym-specific Infusionsoft dashboards were keeping management much more organized about where each contact from their list was in respect to *The Perfect Athlete Life Cycle* stages, which was cuing gym staff to utilize specific systems that encourage acquisition and retention of member athletes.

In addition to this, a great deal of prospect nurturing and client on-ramp automation was in place to take the onus off of each gym's staff, but still ensure that Iron Tribe engagement was being established and maintained for each contact in our database, no matter which stage of *The Perfect Athlete Life Cycle* they were in.

However, as helpful as these two preceding results were, the biggest result was the fact that we went from 83% of our leads "raising their hands of interest" offline in 2011 (phone calls and walk-ins) to 78% of them coming in through the internet (Infusionsoft web forms) in 2012!

This is the ultimate story of marketing becoming "sales in print." Infusionsoft changed our entire conversion system and the rate at which we were converting prospects into new member athletes.

Because the majority of our prospects were being sent to the web, whether it was a direct-response ad or a referral, they

Recommended Resource: Infusionsoft

Dan Kennedy endorses Infusionsoft, and GKIC and many of his clients' business's direct marketing, "no-fail" follow-up marketing, and CRM functions are powered by Infusionsoft. You can learn more and get an online demo of Infusionsoft at www.Infusionsoft.com. Many, many businesses, incidentally, utilize Infusionsoft "off the shelf" with no customization or integration into other platforms. Infusionsoft also provides marketing templates created by Dan Kennedy. A convenient place to meet with Infusionsoft representatives, learn about it, and meet and talk with users is the annual GKIC SuperConference℠ or annual GKIC Info-SUMMIT℠, to which you will automatically receive invitations if taking advantage of the FREE OFFER FROM DAN on page 261.

were becoming educated with the "LIFE. Changed." stories both on the website itself and, once they filled out a web form, via automated follow-up mail and email sequences.

So instead of hearing about Iron Tribe and then calling or walking in to speak to a salesperson, prospects were getting educated about us on demand and on their terms, before the person-to-person sales process ever began.

Once they were convinced of Iron Tribe's validity to transform them from the marketing process, they were cued to call and set up a consultation at the gym closest to them.

The result was a whopping 96% close rate at the consultation table because they come in presold to join the tribe!

Forrest and I thought this test was something special enough to at least apply for the Infusionsoft Ultimate Marketer of the Year award, even though we knew that more than 10,000 businesses around the world use the software, and it'd be tough to actually win the award. However, to our surprise, we not only were selected to present on stage in front of more than 2,000 people, as one of the four finalists for this award, but we were voted the winners!

Winning the award has had an ROI of its own for the franchise model because we were crowned as the winners on the very same day that we officially began franchising. Since then, the award has gotten us more PR and speaking opportunities to grow our expert status and credibility in just one year than most established brands have earned over a much longer time period, with a price tag that we couldn't have afforded.

As for *The Bay Door*, our developers have knocked it out of the park, building tech that our franchisees can utilize to continue growing the Iron Tribe brand within their own tribes. So it is taking the results of this Infusionsoft test and cranking it up to an even higher standard.

The back-end staff UI streamlines staff processes that used to seem tedious to allow their jobs to be focused more on prospect and client engagement and much less on the creative external and internal marketing processes that they'd rather not think about.

The front-end client UIs provide constant brand imprints on the brains of each Iron Tribe athlete through the website, iPad, and iPhone applications. They not only continue to enhance retention but, once again, increase members' ability to refer and help us grow faster than ever.

Oh, yeah, and it gives us a place and automated method to sell them further products and services on top of their monthly athlete membership subscriptions.

You may be able to accomplish a lot of this with basic Infusionsoft or with other technology. Maybe you'll need to band together with other owners and operators of your kind of business to get a customized or semi-customized automated marketing system built. However you have to do it, you'll find that automation of marketing and communications is a game-changer and a great competitive advantage.

Go to www.IronTribeFranchise.com/NoBS to watch Jim Cavale and Forrest Walden provide commentary on this chapter and see real Iron Tribe marketing samples along with a special look inside of The Bay Door software platform!

CHAPTER 10

Faster Than They Can Copy

by Jim Cavale

N o brand dare stand still. We understood from the beginning that we would never get There, wherever There is. Not be able to rest and take a breather. That building a brand was not a journey so much as an endless process.

A lot of brand owners get lazy, and then they get commoditized, and then they are gone. Consider the demise of the venerable Kodak, a brand with roots in the 19th century. At one time, you would have had a difficult time finding any home without Kodak cameras, film, or processed photographs in it. But then, Instagram. And something looming will be next. The difference between a commodity and an engaging experience that fascinates and keeps customers is innovation. The chief cause of commoditization is imitation, then proliferating imitation. The only practical answer is innovation.

We know we can't rely on our brand—unless we keep people interested in it.

Let's Give 'Em Something To Talk About

The latest research shows that people share more than 16,000 words per day and every hour there are more than 100 million conversations about brands. This has put word-of-mouth at the forefront of as much as 50% of all business transactions.

People hear this and immediately think, "Wow, technology has changed the entire game, because people are doing all of this word-of-mouth on the internet."

WRONG.

More than 90% of word-of-mouth marketing actually occurs *offline!*

Iron Tribe has a social status to it. Member athletes feel like they just HAVE to talk about it, whether it's because of their personal transformation, the different things they accomplish in their workouts that most people have never done before, or, of course, the exclusivity and status that come from the premium cost that those on the outside may question.

Each member athlete feels like an insider, as they should. They are working harder together than most on the outside could ever imagine. They are also part of a group that is much bigger than themselves. It creates an insider feeling of exclusivity that has a scarcity to it because there are only 300 member athlete spots per Iron Tribe gym.

These are all motivating factors for their word-of-mouth, and so is the gamification aspect that has each member athlete consistently competing with their own workout results, let alone those of their peers.

However, these are all aspects of our business model that Forrest so eloquently laid the groundwork for with his initial development of the Iron Tribe business model.

It's been a blessing to join him in developing this model over time. And while he and I will continue to enhance all of the preceding aspects of the business model and the overall brand itself, our biggest innovation playground will always revolve around the direct-response marketing portion of our business.

The biggest innovation piece we are working on today is not in our technology or even our unit economics. Instead, it's a business-to-business campaign to provide our gyms with the ability to sell groups of athlete memberships in one consultation to an entire business group of employees who are scared of health-care costs and need a program like Iron Tribe to keep them away from the doctor!

We continue to ask our selves, "How can we get our new gyms to 300 faster?"

The day we stop asking that question is the day we turn toward Kodak-like complacency and away from the innovative tests that have helped us grow to this point.

> **RESOURCES**
>
> **From Jim Cavale and Forrest Walden of Iron Tribe**
>
> Please see page 262 for a free resources offer.
>
> **From Dan Kennedy**
>
> Please see page 261 for a free resources offer.

Hopefully, everything Forrest and I have shared here will inspire lots of varied innovation on your part.

Go to www.IronTribeFranchise.com/NoBS to watch Jim Cavale and Forrest Walden provide commentary on this chapter and see real Iron Tribe marketing samples as well as a video presentation of their new business-to-business direct-mail marketing innovation they've developed and tested since writing this book!

CHAPTER 11

Brand-Building Powered by Unique Selling Proposition and Dynamic Core Story:

GKIC Case Study Examples

by Dave Dee

H ey, it's Dave Dee again. We met earlier in the Preface. One of the things I get to do at GKIC is talk with and coach many of our Members, old and new, during the course of each year, at our two big annual conferences, the Fast Start Implementation Boot Camps held several times a year, in my Platinum Mastermind Group, and on question-answer tele-seminars and webinars. One of the ideas that's just about unanimous with all these business owners I talk to, train, coach, and share information with is a desire to own a great brand. A lot of businesspeople who want one never engage in the kind of thinking we're all involved in now, in this book, about what such a desirable thing, the great brand, is actually made of.

There's a brand you probably know: Intel. Many computer and technology products are labeled and promoted as "Having Intel Inside" or "Powered By Intel." I like the phrase "Powered By." It suggests that there's a force driving things forward, making them possible. Direct-response brand-building and brands are powered by three components: a Unique Selling Proposition (USP), a Dynamic Core Story (DCS), and effective visual presence—which gets to brand image, trademarks, colors, as well as places where you are seen, from the media you choose, to storefront looks, to the charity or community events sponsored. Here we're going to zero in on the first two, and how people in very different businesses have used them as well as some advice I've given them along the way.

Example 1: Shaun Buck, The Newsletter Pro

Shaun is in two GKIC coaching groups, the Peak Performers/Implementation Group and the Titanium Group, after time in my Platinum Group. He is a very ambitious, very creative entrepreneur essentially in the printing business, but made proprietary and un-ordinary by creating customized newsletters for various kinds of businesses and professional practices to send to their customers and patients. His USP is: *Creating unique newsletters, entirely done for you, mailed directly to your customers and prospects for you, that sound as if they were written by you—without you ever having to write a single word, guaranteed.* Shaun has absolutely nailed that USP. It tells his prospects exactly what he does for them, it promises ease and convenience without dull standardization, and it includes mention of a guarantee, all in just 35 words.

Here is his DCS:

> I had my first experience with newsletters when I was looking to purchase my second business. I started

my research by requesting information from a few dozen franchise companies. Along with brochures and franchise documents, I got a lot of phone calls, but, after a month or two, the phone calls had all but stopped. Only one franchisor, selling a dry cleaning business, kept in contact with an 8- to 16-page monthly newsletter. Every time an issue came in the mail, I read it from cover to cover. I couldn't wait to read about the success different franchise owners were having. Over months, I felt like I had a connection with this franchise company and the people in it. When a newsletter arrived all about their coming annual convention, I bought my franchise six months sooner than I'd planned so I could attend. Once I got started operating a franchise dry cleaning store, I found out one of the requirements was that you had to publish a monthly newsletter and send it to all your customers. This made sense because it copied the way I'd been sold my franchise. But, with no training or guidance, I took a stab at my newsletter, and I may have created the world's most boring newsletter! I made mistakes most business owners make trying this—for example, 1) being boring, 2) being entirely focused on my business instead of on my customers and their interests, 3) not seeing the newsletter as a piece of an overall strategy, and 4) not using it to build relationship with my customers.

After two years of struggling, I went back to the newsletters I'd received that I had wanted to read. I reworked my entire newsletter. Less than three days after my first issue of this new, friendly, interesting, relationship-building newsletter went out, I got my first call from a customer raving about it. I jokingly asked her what she thought about the old version, and she said she'd never seen it, even though I had been mailing it to her for two years! We continued to build our business by mailing this newsletter, but I admit I always had a hard time finding the day it took every month to do. When I decided to move on from the dry cleaning business and thought about my best skill, I realized that I had mastered retaining customers and sparking referrals with a great newsletter. That day, Newsletter Pro was born. It's not about teaching you to do it, and it's not about prefabricated, standardized content. I created a company to produce customized and unique newsletters that sound like they are written by you, for your customers, without you having to ever lift a finger or take time away from your business.

Isn't Shaun's DCS great? He has an interesting origin story about how he first discovered the power of newsletters. He also has a struggle-and-triumph story that shows him getting a hard knocks education on how to put together newsletters that work and that suggests to his prospect that there are a lot of mistakes to be avoided by using his services. His DCS positions Shaun as the go-to guy for newsletter marketing.

Example 2: Sandro Piancone, The Mexpert

GKIC Diamond Member Sandro Piancone runs a $100 million-a-year organization that helps companies sell and import their products to Mexico. His USP is *The leading authority to doing business profitably in Mexico, used by some of the world's largest companies.* I think there's an opportunity to make the USP more dramatic and specific: *Step-by-step processes for profitably exporting your consumer packaged goods into the Mexican marketplace without lawyers or international trade hassles — guaranteed.*

DAN KENNEDY'S COMMENT: Dave definitely strengthened the impact of Sandro's USP, with specifics and with problems or fears erased, like "without lawyers." But in my opinion, he sacrificed what I call Leadership Position in the rewrite. My version is: *The leading authority in doing business profitably in Mexico, relied on by some of the world's largest companies for step-by-step processes and successful export of consumer packaged goods into the Mexican marketplace—without lawyers or international trade hassles, guaranteed.* Obviously, mine is more verbose, but still just 39 words. If it can be said as one long or two short sentences, I'm fine with this length of a USP. The key goal is clarity, not just brevity.

Sandro's DCS:

I am the Chief Mexpert Officer of Mexico Sales Made Easy. Yes, Mexpert is a real word. I trademarked it. I'm not a Mexpert because I have a degree in international business or finance, but because, in 14 years, I have made more mistakes than anyone and spent more money making those mistakes than anyone in selling into this market. My team and I can make sure you don't repeat any of those mistakes. While making mistakes, I've also hit home runs and grand slams. Since 1998, I have generated over $500 million in sales and profits for my clients and partners, and I have introduced a number of U.S. brands to Mexico, including Miller Beer, Roma Food, and

Rockstar Energy Drinks. I currently work with Little Caesar's and 5-Hour Energy.

Sandro's DCS establishes authority, credibility, and expertise. It is specific about his years of experiences, sales achievement, and client roster—not vague or general. It's made more believable because he mentions mistakes as well as successes. That also makes Sandro come off as a likable guy—which, incidentally, he is.

Example 3: Al Watson, Fanfare Catering

Al is, as of this book's writing, new to GKIC and to the way we approach marketing. He has quickly made great strides. His USP was: *Fanfares will take your ideas, add our expertise, and create an event you will never forget.* While it's alive with promise, it's a little too general, and it fails to play to Fanfare's coolest asset: they are literally caterers to the stars, which I learned only by talking to Al. The better USP we worked out is: *Caterer to the stars, Al Watson and Fanfares will take your ideas, add our expertise, and create a uniquely customized event that will make you and your guests feel like VIP celebrities.* We've brought Al himself into this, added benefit language (customized), and added emotional appeal, telling them they'll *feel like* celebrities. When Dan Kennedy saw it, he wanted to tinker further because he hated giving up Al's original "never forget" idea. That produced: *Caterer to the stars, Al Watson and Fanfares will take your ideas, add our expertise, and create a uniquely customized event that will make you and your guests feel like VIP celebrities— and that no one will ever forget!*
Al's DCS:

My parents started the company when I was 10 years old. Fanfares started by right place, right time.

My dad was a salesman for C&K Distributors, which sold Old Style Beer, and he was making a sales call at Al Pars Liquors, the one on 71st Street. He overheard Al making arrangements to sponsor a concert, heard him saying he needed a caterer, and Dad yelled, "I'll do it." Al looked at him and asked, "Do you know what you are doing, Ted?" And Dad said, "Of course, done it many times." We did not know what to do. We actually hired another caterer and watched them for the next three months, then really started on our own. We started in the entertainment industry, catering for Patti LaBelle, Rick James, Prince, and many others I can't name. Our staff consisted of Mom and Dad; my grandmother, Mama Jewel; a great-aunt;, and Anne, Mom's play sister. Our waitstaff and dishwashers were me at 10 years old, another 10-year-old, and an 11-, 12-, and 13-year-old. Guests loved it when we were serving, even though I could barely see over the buffet table. They only paid us $20.00 a day for 10-hour days. Our parents didn't care—they wanted their boys working. We were rich in our world! I wish I could get away with that today. Now, when people want a flawless event, they call Fanfares.

I have edited a lot out of Al's DCS. It was far too long and risked being boring. Worse, he focused on his company as he likes to think about it rather than on how his business benefits its customers. When you talk about yourself and your company, you have to connect it to benefits the customers care about. In my rewrite of Al's DCS, you'll see what I've left behind and the additional information I pulled out of him.

My parents Faye and Ted started the company when I was 10 years old. My dad was a salesman for

C&K Distributors, which sold Old Style Beer, and he was making a sales call at Al Pars Liquors, the one on 71st Street. He overheard Al making arrangements to sponsor a concert, heard him saying he needed a caterer, and Dad yelled, "I'll do it." Al looked at him and asked, "Do you know what you are doing, Ted?" And Dad said, "Of course, done it many times." We did not know what to do. We actually hired another caterer and watched them for the next three months, then really started on our own. Our commitment was to create flawless events, not just deliver and serve good food and drink. Because of this, we caught the eye of the entertainment industry and started catering for Patti LaBelle, Rick James, Prince, and many others I can't name. We became known as Caterers to the Stars. We've catered Nelson Mandela's Freedom Tour, private fundraisers for President Clinton, movie shoots for Denzel Washington, national commercial shoots with Morgan Freeman, even President Barack and Michelle Obama's wedding reception. But our mission is not just to serve stars, it's to make all our clients' events unforgettable.

Notice that the story is still charming and has its roots, but focuses on what Fanfares can do for the client. There is tremendous social proof. Before GKIC, Al wasn't mentioning most of the celebrities he's catered for, including President Obama! If you have impressive customers, you definitely want to show them off and use them.

As you can see, it takes time and creative thinking to get to the best possible USP and DCS. This is helped a lot by brainstorming with other smart marketers and qualified coaches, a creative environment that we provide for GKIC

Members, but that you can organize for yourself, too. I don't think you can build or support a great brand without a strong USP and DCS, and I *know* you can't successfully do direct-response advertising and marketing without them. So whatever work and however much time and persistence are needed to get to them, it just has to be done!

CHAPTER 12

A Brand without Marketing Is a Tree Falling in a Distant, Unpopulated Forest

by Steve Adams

Y ou've heard that saying—if a tree falls in a distant, unpopulated forest, and nobody hears it, does it even matter? If a brand has been invested in and had great importance attached to it by its owner, but it isn't effectively marketed, does it matter? Brand or no brand, you'll be in the same place without a marketing system. I'd like to tell you how I came to that understanding, and what I did about it.

It's July 1996, and I've just relocated my family from Michigan to Wisconsin. I'm launching my first entrepreneurial venture after ten years as a commercial loan officer.

After investing ten years of study into the success and leadership literature, and a very successful banking career, I was now in control of a new business of my own. I quickly discovered that nothing in my traditional marketing education and big-company experience prepared me for my biggest challenge in business.

Looking back, it's easy to see that I overvalued brand identity, in this case bought in the form of a franchise. The same mistake can be made creating your own brand identity from scratch. A brand, a brand name, brand identity, logo, slogan—these things are assets and can be valuable assets, but they are not marketing. There's no substitute for marketing!

That first major challenge was insufficient sales. Despite having a franchise flag, the brand was new to the market.

Advertising representatives flooded into my store to pitch their programs for TV, radio, new neighbor kits, Valpak, and community coupon programs. Every charity you can imagine, in and out of the pet-related world, came to the new guy with limited money for advertising and donations. I spent a lot of money on advertising.

For our first grand opening, we ran six radio spots a day on three stations for a week, we ran TV ads and a full-circulation newspaper FSI. We were flooded with new customers, and I thought I was really smart.

Then the trouble began.

Immediately after the grand opening, revenues fell back 40% and significantly below break-even. My immediate response was to sign up for regular radio, newspaper, and coupon book marketing at costs that were not easy to digest, given we were losing money.

As the months went by, sales gradually grew but my frustration grew right along with it. Where were these sales coming from? What if I eliminated some of this marketing to achieve break-even sooner? What would the impact be? No one I knew could tell me the answer. The advertising representatives' answers were always along the lines of "whoever spends the most wins the game."

More than once, we had to cancel a marketing program we signed up for and arrange a payment plan to make good on what we spent because revenues didn't grow and we couldn't afford to continue to spend.

My frustration with this pattern of buy a program, no growth, and cancel reached its peak in 2003 when we had to close two stores in the Dallas-Fort Worth market. We entered the market in 2001 and had disastrous results. Our biggest problem, again, was an unknown brand, which translated into very slow adoption rates of our stores by new pet owners. There was no shortage of pet owners in Texas. They just didn't know or trust us.

At the height of my frustration with advertising, I quit. I quit all advertising and informed our team we were going to work on our business model and become so good at what we did that word-of-mouth alone would generate the growth. In the meantime, I cut 100% of our advertising spend and downsized store count until we were profitable; then I immediately went to work on reinventing our value proposition.

Our franchise, at that point, was a loosely tied group of store owners who had license to do as we pleased with product, real estate, and marketing. The deal was to pay the fees, run a good, clean store, and go about building our business. The primary value-add was the monthly ad circular and buying power the franchise had given us.

We were the first franchisee to enter a major metropolitan market as the third entrant. The problem was we showed up with a generic selling proposition. This was THE reason for poor sales results. Pet owners saw no compelling reason to choose us over all the other options they had to purchase pet supplies.

We entered 2004 with the goal of creating a new Unique Selling Proposition (USP) for the company. Our process was to map out what our competitors focused on and then determine what we could do much better that didn't match their USP focal points.

Our choices were: 1) expertise of the staff, 2) quality of our staff interactions, and 3) emphasis on organic and natural foods and supplies. Later, through the influence of Dan Kennedy, this transitioned to differentiating on how we sell our clients, the experience they have in the store, and the expertise of our store personnel. Our overall positioning is that of "trusted authority."

For the next several years, we experienced steady growth rates of 6% to 8%. We upgraded our store personnel through hiring profiles and providing generalized pet-care training. Word-of-mouth marketing was working. We provided a good experience in the stores. Our team had good solutions for pet owners who were tired of the "know-nothing" employees at our major chain competitors.

During the period of 2004–2008, we grew to four stores, and in mid-June 2008, we completed an acquisition of five stores in Birmingham/Tuscaloosa, Alabama. After the acquisition, we upgraded the staff, invested in pet-care training, and continued with the zero marketing investment mind-set.

It also was during this period that the infamous pet food recall occurred due to lethal chemicals being found in food manufactured in China. We were inundated with frightened pet owners asking us if we knew if their food was safe. Fortunately for us, one of our customers in Dallas was a reporter for the Dallas Fox News affiliate. She knew our team had a higher level of expertise than the typical pet store so she interviewed one of our managers in the midst of the recall crisis. Sales immediately jumped 10% in our two Texas stores.

I realized at that moment that an opportunity for truly unique positioning was staring me right in the eyes. What if we could be recognized as the leading experts in every market regarding pet nutrition? Every dog and cat has to eat, so this was a big issue that we could become the "go to" place for answers.

In 2009, I was able to develop and implement a nutrition certification program with Dr. Sarah Abood, DVM Ph.D., the lead nutrition professor at Michigan State University's School of Veterinary Medicine. Today we have more than 100 certified pet nutritionists in our 21 stores giving great advice to pet owners each day.

Then in 2010, revenues flattened to zero growth across our entire ten-store group in Alabama, Texas, and Wisconsin. I realized I needed to make a key executive change and step into direct market leadership.

I simplified a lot of the operational processes and harmonized our merchandise assortments and loyalty program with a now active and value-creating franchisor. We also improved our overall internal store culture.

The importance of marketing that internal store culture and professionalism cannot be overstated. Great direct-response marketing will accelerate the demise of a poorly run retail business.

However, it was then that I realized being a better merchant, becoming more operationally sound, tinkering endlessly with store design and real estate could only do so much. The first half of 2010 revenues *declined* on a same-store basis by 5%. However, through the previously mentioned changes, we were back to 3% to 4% positive sales comps by the fourth quarter of that year. Overall, we suffered through our first flat sales growth year since early in the decade.

The improvements made in 2010 bore fruit in 2011. Those improvements generated our best revenue growth year ever with companywide sales increasing 10% for the year. As the fall approached, I knew we needed something else to continue this growth. The 2011 bump was event driven around some clearly identifiable improvements—inside the store—that would not be able to generate consistent growth year after year on its own.

If we were going to become a company that grew above the industry norm year after year, we needed to learn to become marketers. I was still an advertising victim, so rather than return to old patterns, I began to do some research.

I met fellow author and entrepreneur Tony Rubleski through a mutual friend one day in my office. Tony reached out to meet again, and we met over coffee at Starbucks. At the end of the meeting, I offered my credit card to Tony and asked him to send me $250.00 of his best marketing information that I could read to help me.

I wasn't someone who liked to enter into consulting retainer agreements. I wanted to do my own independent thinking first, then once I achieved a level of mastery, would hire consultants to leverage my effectiveness.

In that package was my introduction to Dan Kennedy. I don't even remember the other items in the box. I read the book *No B.S. Direct Marketing for Non-Direct Marketing Businesses* and was instantly hooked.

I signed up for GKIC Gold Membership, read both *The Ultimate Marketing Plan* and *The Ultimate Sales Letter*, and within 60 days, had crafted our first four-page sales letter. A compiled list, suppressed against our current customer base, was purchased, and the letter was sent late in November 2011.

That first sales letter, and one reactivation postcard with concepts learned from Dan, had an immediate impact. We sent out 4,000 letters and received 206 new clients into our stores! More amazing was our reactivation postcard that had nearly a 70% response. It was the best holiday season we had ever experienced.

At that moment, I became a Dan Kennedy convert and bought nearly every book he had published. I read all of them over a two-month period. I realized for the first time that I needed to become a professional marketer of my business and less a doer of my business.

After attending a GKIC Implementation Boot Camp in Atlanta, Georgia, with my IT Director, who is now my Marketing Director, it became clear that we could, in fact, control our own destiny through a systematic plan to grow revenues.

Marketing by Numbers

The first thing we did was build a data warehouse and create a flow of information to the database from our loyalty program and point-of-sale systems so that we could understand our marketing math.

We learned what our first-year client profit was and began to base marketing investment decisions off that metric. We chose gross profit because we have to remove product cost from annual revenues to calculate what we can pay to acquire a new client. Additionally, we chose first-year rather than lifetime value because we didn't want to assume long retention periods given the dynamics of retailing.

In retailing with multiple stores, volume is a challenge in designing marketing programs. Whatever we came up with had to be scalable across multiple stores and markets. Furthermore, I wanted to acquire new clients, retain the clients we had, increase frequency and annual client spend, and finally, begin to regularly reactivate lost clients.

New Client Acquisition

For acquisition, we contracted with Craig Simpson of Simpson Direct to help us acquire the right mailing lists based on our best client profile and to manage the overall process of getting a monthly sales letter out in multiple markets. Craig is also invaluable in testing new concepts, format design, and copy review.

Additionally, we hired Kevin Donlan, a Dan Kennedy-trained copywriter, to improve upon my original sales letter to create a control we could mail out month after month with success.

Earlier, I mentioned an aversion to hiring consultants. I made the time investment in studying direct-response marketing, understood the fundamentals, and now, given our scale, needed the help of experts to leverage my time and accelerate our results.

I see entrepreneurs unwilling to spend money with people who can help them get to where they want to be. They fail to make the connection of greater profits sooner offsetting the cost of the consultants.

> **RESOURCES**
>
> Craig Simpson is an expert in list selection and procurement and all things direct mail, functions as a freelance direct-mail project manager, and publishes the *Mailbox Millionaire* newsletters. Information at www.Simpson-Direct.com. His book, published by Entrepreneur Press, *The Direct-Mail Solution*, co-authored with Dan Kennedy, is available at all booksellers.

That Was Then, This Is Now

That tells you about the early journey, during which a banker bought a brand and became a retailer, but had to learn that neither a good brand nor a good retailing operation is enough. That was then. This is what drives our 21-store chain now . . .

Armed with help from these outstanding experts, we now mail a monthly four-page sales letter in a self-mailer format. The letter emphasizes our trusted authority positioning with the elements of a good sales letter. Over the past year, the average response is 1.78% with 2,399 new clients acquired and an average ROI of 271%.

An additional acquisition strategy we employ is an alliance referral program with animal rescues and partner businesses. We offer a $25.00-off coupon to first-time clients who have adopted a pet or are first-time clients referred by business partners. It's a value-add to our partner clients. We then pay the rescue referral a donation of $20.00 for each redemption and $10.00 to our business partners.

Through the first full year of the alliance referral program, we acquired 6,776 new clients. The overall ROI on the program the first year was 173%.

There's Gold in the List

Another challenge every business has, but few grasp, is growth through marketing to the house file. Before entering Dan's world, we were no different. We had more than 350,000 buyers in our database, and we were doing nothing to increase our share of wallet with them.

In retail, it is common for consumers to cross-shop a store with direct competitors. They follow advertised specials. We wanted to escape that commodity trap, so we invested in our nutrition certification program. It's an extensive web-based pet-care university tool and leadership/client facing engagement training. We were positioning ourselves as experts and being the trusted authority.

Now, our marketing challenge was to learn how to market this positioning effectively to our client base. We wanted to cause them to consolidate purchases with our stores, which would lead to increased frequency and spend.

We chose a combination of education and old-fashioned bribery. Our retention and frequency enhancement marketing plan consists of the following:

1. Monthly printed eight-page newsletter to our top 500 clients per store. FSI (Free Standing Insert) is embedded into the newsletter. We haven't determined how to measure an ROI on this yet; however, we believe enough reasons exist to continue sending it to our best clients.

2. Three holiday postcards per year to our "A" segment clients with a 10%-off offer as a thank you. Our 2013 Valentine's Day holiday card generated an 18.44% response, an average transaction size lift of 28%, and a 417% ROI net of all costs and discounts.

3. A quarterly educational upsell sales letter using the classic buyers of "x" who don't buy "y" concept. Examples include dental health, puppy food buyers not purchasing chew toys, dog buyers not buying flea and tick medications, etc.

   - The puppy product upsell letter generated a 6.19% response, an average transaction size lift of 35.79%, and an ROI of 56 %.

   - An upsell letter on fleas and ticks was a tremendous success with 23.02% response, 23.41% transaction lift, and an ROI of 683%.

4. Annual anniversary thank-you letter with a 20% Off Shopping Spree check attached. This program average is 34.36% response, transaction size lift of 39.74%, and ROI of 285% net of the discount and all fulfillment costs.

5. Three annual holiday cards to top 500 "B" segment clients with a 10%-off offer to move them up to "A" segment clients. This is a new tactic that was recently mailed and the returns are not known as this point.

6. Annual pet birthday postcard program. This is a program administered by the franchiser. We have no marketing math on this strategy. We are in the process of pulling that back to our company where it will be measured.

> **RESOURCES**
>
> Examples of all the marketing campaigns Steve Adams is using to implement these six parts of his marketing program can be seen at http://www.PassionateEntrepreneur.com/brand.

As I write this, we are only in the early stages of building out a much more comprehensive program that will multiply the number and combination of offers going to existing clients throughout each year.

 DAN KENNEDY'S COMMENT: My friend and speaking colleague, a great success philosopher, the late Jim Rohn said, "If you follow a highly successful person in any field around for a week, there will be no mystery about why he is doing so well. You'll say to yourself, 'Well, look at EVERYTHING he does.'" Because Steve is in my highest level mastermind/coaching group at GKIC, the Titanium Group, I get the opportunity to see what he implements and achieves

---

DAN KENNEDY'S COMMENT, continued

in between our three-times-a-year meetings. I can assure you, if you followed Steve as I do, you'd have the reaction Jim Rohn described five times over. Steve has just described, and is going to continue to describe, A LOT OF things he's doing to drive new customers into his stores and, importantly, his system, and to then keep them interested and engaged, and to sell more to them by consolidating all their pet-related purchasing under his roof. Having such a complete system is, bluntly, more valuable and more important than having a cool or clever or even famous brand. It is also, admittedly, more work than relying on brand. Having such a system empowers you to derive the greatest value from a brand. If everything he's describing seems overwhelming, take note of the fact that he built it over time, not overnight, that he is in continuous development and improvement, that he has organized a small but mighty support team around him (on staff and outside experts), and that he is all about putting marketing in place that has ongoing or evergreen use (not one-time promotions). This is the difference between "building" versus just "doing."

Reactivating Lost Clients

I often share a metaphor with our store teams. Growing each store is like trying to fill a water bucket with a hole in the bottom.

If the bucket already has water in it, this is analogous to existing sales. Through acquisition efforts such as sales letters, FSIs, and alliance marketing programs, we turn the hose on and fill the bucket.

Through retention marketing efforts that increase share of wallet and frequency, we also increase the water line in the bucket. The problem is our bucket has a hole in the bottom that lowers the water line or sales. That is called "customer churn" in retailing.

Our strategy to remedy this problem is twofold. First, the experience in the store cannot act to make the hole bigger. We have a specific set of strategies to guarantee that each of our clients has a great experience.

The second part of plugging the hole in the bottom is to have a systematic program for reactivating lost clients. Our system is a three-step series of humorous postcards developed by Dean Killingbeck's New Customers Now team in Howell, Michigan. Go to www.PassionateEntrepreneur.com/brand to view this hilarious, yet effective, series of postcards to bring lost clients back into our stores.

The performance of this program has been outstanding. I will share an actual three-step campaign from February–April 2013. The first month (February) we sent postcard No. 1, and 1,514 clients reactivated for a 43.47% response. They spent $56,690.00. The next month (March) we sent postcard No. 2, and that generated another 215 clients who did not respond to the first postcard. That was another 14.14% with a total of $5,632.00 spent. The third month (April) we sent the third postcard to those who did not respond to the first two. We reactivated another 109 clients from that original February list for another 13.71% in response and $3,421.00 in total spend.

So, for the entire campaign we reactivated 1,838 clients who spent $60,743.00. When we subtracted out the mailing and coupon costs, our net profit on the sum of the return transactions was $2,273.00. However, assuming only half of our typical first-year profit after product costs of $175.00, given their propensity to churn, the program delivered $161,744.00 of first-year profit against $21,193.00 of total costs for a 763% ROI.

An additional reactivation strategy we use is scripted calls. Each month, each store manager is supplied a report of his or her "A" and "B" segment clients who have churned. Their job, using a script, is to call as many as they can each month (minimum requirement is all "A" segment clients) and say sorry and find out how they can recover them. It is an educational process for them, and it heightens their awareness of this critical issue.

After an intense 18 months, we have a system that works every aspect of the water bucket. Our marketing system generates new clients, increases frequency and client spend, and reactivates lost clients month after month.

Changing Your Economics

One of the principles Dan teaches is to monetize your client list, which then becomes a back-end revenue source to your primary business revenue model. Successfully building a back end then changes the economics of your business and enables you to pay more to acquire and retain clients.

Those businesses that can delay profit the longest when acquiring clients or which can spend the most to retain their best clients are in the greatest position to win in the crowded marketplace. It's the way Main Street businesses can win against the category killers, Walmarts and other behemoth corporations.

At our company, we have a large database of buyers. We have detailed transactional history on them as well as multiple demographic and psychographic characteristics appended by client in the system.

We have a large opportunity to build a back-end revenue business model on top of our core Main Street brick-and-mortar business. Additionally, building the back end reinforces our positioning as a trusted authority.

Our back end consists of four revenue funnels: 1) paid membership, 2) how-to audio and video products with starter kits, 3) a box-of-the-month club for dogs, and 4) auto-ship of orders.

The membership program provides valuable content in the form of expert interviews, an expanded content printed newsletter, annual nutrition exams, and other benefits. A certain percentage of our clients want more education to be better pet parents. This program provides that education.

The how-to products are videos of our staff experts demonstrating how to do things such as brush a dog's teeth as well as assess and treat common ear, eye, skin, and coat problems. We also teach how to trim nails. Another program teaches the basics of animal nutrition. All the programs are bundled with product to then implement what the client has learned.

Our box-of-the-month club is essentially like book-of-the-month clubs except the contents are a surprise. Our www.dawgbox.com is a website that gives the dog owner the opportunity to select a small-, medium-, or large-dog box and whether it's for their dog or a gift for another. Then it simply ships each month. We have set it up as a "pay to play" program where vendors contribute to the box to bring value to the client. Again, it's another opportunity to market to our list and extend our reach into our markets and gain new clients.

Finally, our auto-ship program is meant to defend against Amazon, increase frequency of low-frequent category clients, and offer a new option to those who haven't responded to reactivation attempts. We also will prospect in areas outside our typical trade areas to gain incremental revenue and cross-sell our stores and other back-end products. This program is under development and expected to launch in the fourth quarter of 2013.

Create Your Destiny

Since arriving on Planet Dan, I've learned that I CAN change what is possible in my business.

When we've finished implementing our back-end revenue model, our business will literally be a fortress in the marketplace.

Our stores have a continual flow of new clients, we are increasing the value of our existing retail clients through retention marketing, and each month we are consistently recapturing lost clients.

Now with a powerful back end monetizing our house list and providing another avenue to acquire new clients, our economics are changing for the better. No longer am I worried about every competitor who enters my trade area nor do I fret about Amazon and every other internet retailer. No longer am I trapped in commodity hell, focused on the next item and price promotion. My business is a powerful marketing system that cannot be easily copied or defeated.

At this point, I should say that our systems and how we develop our people and our culture all are critical pieces to our success. Without them our marketing would not work in the long run. However, our marketing is the "killer app," if you will, that was the game-changer in our growth the past two years.

What were our overall results? In just 30 months, we grew from 10 stores to 21. Our total revenue grew 85% and employee base from 150 to more than 400. Same-store sales growth in retail is good if you achieve 5%. In 2012 our same-store sales growth for the company as a whole was 14% and through the first half of 2013 remains at 12% to 19%, depending on the month.

If you own a retail store, your job is to go to work on your reason for being. Why should people choose to shop with you?

My advice is to learn how you can become the expert in your space. Then hire the right people, build a culture, and create systems that ensure your client's experience is consistent with each visit. Finally, go build a marketing system and back end that consistently markets your expertise and the unique experience you provide. Then invest in executing on the plan month after month.

STEVE ADAMS operates exceptionally successful retail stores across the country, under the auspices of a national brand, but fueled by direct-response marketing. His retail business can be seen at www.AskPSP.com. He is also involved in e-commerce, information publishing and marketing, and consulting. His book, *The Passionate Entrepreneur,* presents essential, experience-based building blocks for entrepreneurial success. www.PassionateEntrepreneur.com.

DAN KENNEDY'S COMMENT: On the following pages, a few samples of Steve's great direct-response advertising and marketing. First, you see a two-sided, oversized postcard (Figure 12.1 on page 119) with the $21.00 Gift Card Offer, plus the free nutrition consultation, and free report. You can see the PET SUPPLIES PLUS branding throughout the piece, but the emphasis is on direct-response advertising elements: specific reasons why this brand-name store is best, a Unique Selling Proposition ("no other pet store has . . ."), customer testimonials, guarantee, and, of course, the offer. If you compare this to other chains who place their emphasis on their brand, you'll find most of these elements missing or minimized, and instead almost all the "real estate" on their direct-mail pieces is given to brand identity and logo, manufacturers' brand names, and a coupon. And if you ran a pure split-test of their brand/image postcard vs. Steve's direct-response postcard, his wins by wide margin. Next you'll see a

DAN KENNEDY'S COMMENT, continued

slightly different version of this postcard, personalized to the recipient in the headlines on both sides of the postcard.

The "Is Your Dog Suffering In Silence?" newspaper ad (Figure 12.2 on page 120)—also useful as a direct-mail piece noted as a reprint from the publication—has almost no branding. Obviously it is set up as an article, called "an advertorial," not a graphic or pictorial ad. Big companies usually can't bear to "bury the brand" with this kind of advertising despite its effectiveness, so the small-business operator can find competitive advantage here. The warning is: Don't muck it up by plastering brand identity, logo, slogan onto it—top, side, middle, bottom, anywhere.

Finally, there's a postcard sent only to new puppy owners (Figure 12.3, page 121.) It carries the brand name front and back, but the emphasis is on the message and the offer.

Steve is actually a Unique Selling Proposition marketer more than a Brand Marketer, which is a strategic decision to be made, considering a number of factors, including the established strength of a brand. In Chapter 13, you'll hear from Bill Gough about the use of the very well-established brand Allstate.

To see a complete collection of Steve's samples, visit www.PassionateEntrepreneur.com. To become a GKIC Gold Member and get full access to all my resources as Steve explained he did, take me up on the FREE OFFER on page 261.

FIGURE 12.1: Steve Adams Oversized Postcard

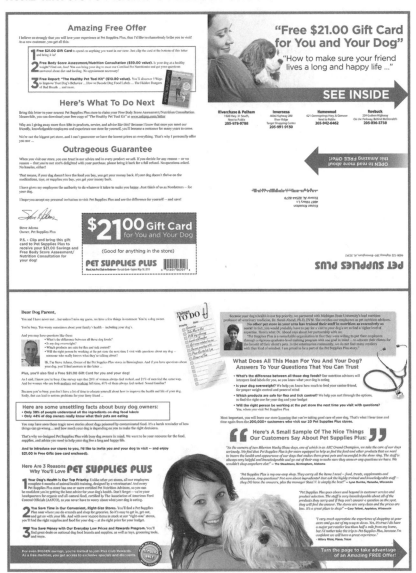

FIGURE 12.2: Steve Adams Newspaper Ad

BIRMINGHAM HEALTH NEWS TODAY — Friday, March 8, 2013 . B3

Is Your Dog Suffering in Silence?

* * *

How to Avoid This "Silent Killer" and
Help Your Dog Live up to 5 Years Longer

Birmingham, AL. -- When Cindy Franklin's two dogs fought over a bone one night, she had to rush 9-year-old Ginger to the pet clinic. She knew Ginger needed stitches for her mouth, but the veterinarian had a nasty surprise for Cindy.

"The vet was worried about Ginger's gums. One of her teeth had been knocked out in the fight, and she needed minor surgery. But because Ginger had advanced gum disease, the doctor was worried the surgery might not even heal. I never knew that dental care was so important," she said.

The facts show, Cindy's dog is not alone. A shocking 80% of all dogs show signs of gum disease by age 3, according to the American Veterinary Dental Society.

Gum disease begins when bacteria and saliva combine to form plaque, a sticky film on the surface of teeth. Bacteria in plaque can invade the gum tissue, leading to inflamed, bleeding gums.

As gum disease progresses, bacteria in your dog's mouth can enter the bloodstream, causing infections, organ failure, even death.

The Silent Killer

Your dog's life could be shortened up to 5 years by gum disease-related infections, according to Purdue University research.

And because dogs instinctively mask pain to hide weakness from predators, the danger signs can be hard to detect.

"Your dog can't tell you she's in pain, but there are warning signs to look out for," says Steve Adams, Owner of Pet Supplies Plus in Birmingham.

"Watch for bad breath, drooling, and tooth loss, all of which can be signs of dental problems."

"In addition, dogs with gum disease may show a loss of interest in food or toys, and they may resist being touched near the mouth," Adams says.

3 Ways to Protect
Your Dog's Health

Adams offers 3 tips for busy dog owners who want to help their canine friends stay healthy.

"First, choose dental diet-approved food and treats. These can keep your dog's mouth healthy by scrubbing the teeth as they chew," says Adams. Other foods have additives to help keep plaque soft, so it won't form rock-hard tartar.

Second, stock up on chew toys. "The abrasive action in good chew toys can help avoid dental disease," says Adams. Look for rubber balls, Kongs, or thin, bendable rawhide.

Finally, look for approved mouth rinses. "These contain chlorhexidine or other ingredients that help kill bacteria in your dog's mouth."

Slow Economy Boosts
Need for "Plus" Pet Stores

Pet health experts will tell you that, by choosing a pet store that provides nutritional advice in addition to quality pet food and products, you can help your dog live a long, happy life. "Pet Supplies Plus is a remarkable organization in that they were willing to put their employees through a rigorous graduate-level training community. In the veterinarian community, we do not find many retailers with that kind of mindset," says Dr. Sarah Abood, Professor of Veterinary Medicine at Michigan State University.

Dr. Sarah Abood

As a public service, Pet Supplies Plus has agreed to offer a Free Nutrition Consultation to readers of this publication, for a limited time.

"The dangers of dental disease are very real for your dog, but they can largely be prevented. My staff can show you how," says Adams.

While there is no substitute for a visit to the veterinarian, Pet Supplies Plus offers health tips and advice not found in other stores.

"During the Free Nutrition Consultation that we're offering, you can bring your dog to meet our Certified Pet Nutritionist and get your questions answered about diet and feeding."

"And if we spot a dental health issue with your dog, we'll let you know right away, so you can talk to your vet," says Adams.

Free Nutrition Consultation

In addition to a Free Nutrition Consultation readers are eligible to receive two extras from Pet Supplies Plus: a Free $21.00 Gift Card to spend on anything in the store, and a Free Report: *The Healthy Pet Tool Kit.*

"Why am I giving away products, services, and advice? As a dog owner myself, I know that your little friend is a big part of your family. So I want to do everything I can to help dogs lead longer, happier lives," says Adams.

To receive a Free $21 Gift Card, Free Nutrition Consultation, and Free Report, bring this article to your nearest Pet Supplies Plus store before April 6, 2013. You can find the nearest Pet Supplies Plus by going to: **www.mypspstore.com**
Article Code: 909576

FIGURE 12.3: Steve Adams Puppy Postcard

Pet Supplies Plus

Get Your New Puppy On The Right Track and Steer Clear of A "Life Of Crime" During The Dreaded "Puppy Phase"!

Receive 20% OFF Your Next Purchase Plus A FREE Nutritional Assessment! But Hurry! This Offer Expires On March 28, 2013!

June-

Congratulations on being a new puppy parent. We hope you're enjoying the excitement and fun that only a puppy can bring. However, along with the joys there are also some challenges... like accidents, chewing, nipping, barking, and the list goes on. We've taken the time to answer some of the most common questions new puppy parents have and are offering you a FREE Nutritional Assessment and a special deal on your next purchase at Pet Supplies Plus!

WANTED

Slipped out of her collar and enjoyed a night on the town... naked.

The Puppy Phase: It always starts with the seemingly harmless nipping, proceeds to gnawing, which turns into destructive chewing, and always ends up with your good silverware missing and strange dogs hanging around late at night...

At Pet Supplies Plus, our expertly trained staff can answer all your questions about your new puppy... from food to treats, or toys to daily care. Just stop in and ask our Certified Pet Nutrition Advisors... and be sure to bring your new puppy!!!

Over for details!

June Cleaver
725 Mason Rd
Howell, MI 48843

Pet Supplies Plus

20% OFF
your entire purchase!
Hurry! Offer ends 03/28/13!!
Visit askpsp.com/stores for a location near you!
Offer code 909574

June... Bring In This Postcard For Your 20% Savings AND Also Receive A FREE Puppy Nutrition Assessment (valued at $50)!

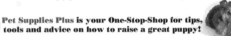

Pet Supplies Plus is your One-Stop-Shop for tips, tools and advice on how to raise a great puppy!

Answers To Three Of The Most Common Questions From Puppy Parents, Just Like You!

Question #1 "What type of treats should I give my puppy? My neighbor fed her puppy treats containing artificial colors. Now her puppy is skipping obedience school and stays out late with the local strays. Are artificial colors a "gateway" to other bad habits and behaviors? How can I make sure that what I'm giving my pup won't harm her?" Marilyn K, puppy parent of "Midge"
Marilyn, great question! First of all, there is no correlation between artificial colors and skipping obedience school, but we understand your concern for your pup's health. We have a huge selection of healthy treats available for your puppy. For example, freeze-dried chicken (or other meat) is great because it's already in small bites! Whatever treat you choose, choose wisely and stay away from treats with Artificial Colors, Wheat, Soy, Corn or Corn Syrup, and meat fat preserved with BHA, which can cause cancer.

Question #2 "What toys are good for my puppy? My pup has turned into a shark and chews everything in sight. As of today, no one in my family owns a pair of matching socks, my son's sneakers look like they were hit with a lawn mower, and my daughter is waiting patiently for her favorite earring to "reappear" in the yard. Help!" Ann F, puppy parent of "Elroy"
Ann, it sounds like your puppy is teething and possibly a bit bored... don't worry, we can help! Look for toys that are designed to alleviate boredom or toys that require your pup to work for treats. Also, invest in some chew toys that will satisfy your puppy's chewing urges, like Nylabones and fleece toys. Both are great options to help your puppy develop his jaw muscles, without redecorating your house or buying a whole new wardrobe for your family. Stop on by and see our huge selection and talk with an expert on what would work best for your pup.

Question #3 "What training aides are best for my puppy? Some of my neighbors have raised the RUDEST puppies, and I want to make sure that my adorable puppy stays adorable and loved by everyone. What steps can I take to raise an obedient, polite puppy who everyone will enjoy being around, including me!" Dana J, puppy parent of "Bella"
Dana, there several areas to consider when raising your puppy to become a cherished member of your family, the top three being: 1) Crate Training; 2) Trimming your dog's nails; and 3) Leashing. Obviously, trimming your pup's nails is a must to stop those scratches, snags and gouges, and helps with proper hygiene and can be a time for bonding . Crate training and leashing are both tools you can use to promote good behavior while giving you and your pup a sense of safety.

CHAPTER 13

Life as a Direct-Response Marketer Under the Umbrella of a Big Brand

by Bill Gough

I have spent most of my business life with the advantage so many entrepreneurs and business owners aspire to and envy: a big, almost universally recognized national brand. My local business operates under its national umbrella of brand, brand advertising on TV, radio, and print, and in online media, with name, logo, and slogan presented to the public every hour of every day. In fact, you probably know Allstate's slogan, even though you certainly made no attempt to memorize it. It's not like there's a test. All I have to say is "You're in Good Hands with" and you'll probably get an A, and correctly name Allstate.

I have been an employee, independent contractor, and an insurance agency owner with this Fortune 100 company since 1984. They are the largest publicly held property and casualty insurer, with the most recognized brand and most famous slogan in the industry.

I'm happy to have had this life under their big-brand umbrella. But it is not my most important asset.

The biggest advantage you have as a business owner and entrepreneur is the *relationships* you have with your customers, prospects, and centers of influence (COIs). It took me many years into my business career for me to learn this most valuable lesson.

How I learned this lesson, and how I've made it the cornerstone of my business, is, I hope you wind up agreeing with, a story worth telling.

One of the big reasons I decided to go to work as an employee insurance agent selling auto, home, and life insurance for Allstate at the tender age of 23 was because of this famous brand. I mean, even I had heard of Allstate, and almost everyone needs or must buy auto and homeowners insurance, right? This should be a piece of cake. I was to be paid nicely plus given an incredible employee benefit package for taking orders for this huge well-known corporation and their famous brand.

I immediately bought into the home office advertising; after all, they were paying for half of it with their generous co-op advertising program for all different media, newspaper, radio, and TV. The local advertising reps were having a field day with all of us working as Allstate agents at the booth at the Sears department store. We were told by the local media reps we needed to "get our name out there," and we followed their "expert" advice until our co-op funds were depleted. As I learned later, these local advertising and media reps are good at one thing, selling their products. I can count on one hand the number I have met in my business career that understand direct-response marketing and true measurement of return of investment (ROI).

Even though I had no way of knowing my results of this traditional image advertising, all sickness is not death. I had one huge advantage as a new agent in Florence, Alabama. I had a real asset in having a REAL business mentor and coach with my Allstate sales manager, Kathy Honaker. She had me working hard in the trenches on some real good things that other top agents in her market were doing with success and holding me accountable for my actions in pursuit on my goals. Most importantly, still used today, and now taught to other insurance agency owners by me today, Kathy taught me how to write out my *goals*, write out business *plans* for their achievement, and, most importantly, do the required *action* of starting the work immediately and being flexible to change toward said goals. I know this is not real earth-shattering news to most of you, but are you doing this?

I finished strong, my first year, winning rookie agent of the year in Alabama and a top 20% in country ranking in the first two years. This was my start in the "real world" just after graduating college with, of all things, degrees from the business school in marketing and management. The next 25 years I was an employee Allstate agent and an Allstate agency owner as an independent contractor with multiple locations. These years were full of a lot of wins, a few losses, and a devastating family tragedy.

For the next few years after losing my mentor to promotion, I also went through a divorce; got into self-pity, excuse making; lost my business drive; and goofed around a lot being single, carefree, and playing a lot of poker. Yeah, that's right, poker. I have played with many of those celebrity guys and gals you see on TV today. No top of the Allstate productions list for me in those days. The best thing I did was manage to keep my job by staying in the middle Allstate agent rankings. Not hard to do when our world accepts so much mediocrity.

After enough of this "play time," I began to hang out with the better agents in our market, started moving up the production leaderboard, and moved into the top 15% to 20% in the country ranking. In just a couple more years in the early 1990s I started hanging out with some of the top 5% of Allstate agency owners and became one of them rather quickly. Once I got there, I stayed at this elite level until I sold the last of my agencies in 2012 to concentrate full time on helping insurance agency owners grow and creating a family legacy through a company I founded in 2008, BGI Marketing Systems.

The top 5% ranking for Allstate agency owners is well rewarded with the highest cash bonuses, more money for approved marketing expenses, plus extra co-op advertising dollars, a very special business meeting of just your peers, and the annual international trip to some of the best destinations and five-star hotels in the world. My wife Vanessa and I have some incredible memories along with lots of Allstate family friends recorded in scrapbooks we will always treasure from Allstate taking us around the world in first-class style.

One thing that I have always done, and it is the biggest shortcut I am aware of toward success, is to watch and learn what really top performers do in their field and emulate it. I am amazed and frankly appalled at the number of people that think they need to do it, whatever "it" is, their own way. To me, this is far more than just ignorance. Ignorance can be fixed, but this stubborn, do-it-yourself activity borders on stupidity. And we are surrounded by it.

Direct-Response Marketing and Two Major Breakthroughs

I was introduced into the world of direct-response marketing in 2004. After networking and hanging out with hundreds of Allstate's very best agency owners for more than a decade and a half, I was no longer an employee agent with Allstate. I now had an independent contractor status with no employee benefits. I was basically a small-business owner and would now be able to sell my agency, along with being able to start and buy more agencies. I was looking for something new or fresh, and, boy, did I find it with Dan Kennedy. Networking with Allstate's best agency owners took me only so far, and there is no school of marketing at Allstate other than the corporate image-based ads. This is the reason for co-op advertising programs that I had long ago learned is me paying half to advertise the famous brand. After all, Allstate's and other major corporations' big advantage is their brand, and they protect that image by controlling the marketing and advertising messages.

I became a serious student of marketing for small-business owners, learning more and more about direct-response marketing and all that it entails. I began marketing the Bill Gough All American Insurance Agency, first using direct-response techniques and leveraging the powerful strength of the Allstate brand behind this new positioning. Almost immediately I began climbing into the 1% to 2% of all 11,000-plus Allstate agency owners in the country. This may not sound like much of a bump from the top 5% to the top 1%, but it is big on many levels, including cash bonus enhancements, company recognition, and tons of valuable high-level perks.

Because of the time spent running the agency and my obsession with this newfound information that, as you know, is about progress, not perfection, other areas of my life were suffering. I was not a very good parent or husband to my family. Thank God I happened to really hear Vanessa say one day calmly, but sternly, "Bill, you don't know much about your three children." She was right, I knew it, and I wanted to change it as the best years of parenting were passing me by.

So I began working on building better systems for more autonomy in my business to free my time to enjoy my family. Similar to what Ray Kroc did to make McDonald's the most successful franchised business in the world, Is for running the day-to-day operations of the agency years ago. I also had my staff in specialized teams of sales, service, and administration, and I was in charge of marketing.

Something I discovered that is very important is that no matter how famous or powerful your brand is, it won't sell itself. And it's not a system. A business, with or without a great brand, that requires you as its chief-everything—chief salesman, chief producer, chief operations person—actually isn't a good business. It's a bad job, however well paid—the kind of bad job that punishes you and your family. A big virtue of a direct-response marketing-driven business is that it can actually be systemized. The obtaining of customers can be systemized. The retention of customers can be systemized.

Two big changes I made really made a huge difference in production, efficiency, and morale. First, promoting managers in each department versus our old style of one office manager for all three departments was the biggest change. Our management team worked together really well as the two ladies promoted in sales and service departments really wanted more responsibility. My former office manager had been stretched thinly over three departments. I had also been freed up to work closely with our three managers, and concentrate on the marketing of our business. Next, I gave ownership to the entire daily tasks outlined in our process manuals to all team members, giving everyone more responsibility in the business. I put in more measurements, and everyone was held accountable for their responsibilities.

An amazing thing happened: Our ranking in Allstate moved inside the top 50 as we improved our business. I was working fewer hours, but I was working on the *right* activities. So now I had more time to spend with my family and friends. All of this happened so quickly from late 2004 to 2006. I had been in business for 20 years, and very successful for most of those years, but in less than two years felt as if I had accomplished more than all of those other years.

January 1, 2007 . . . Worst Day of My Life

As parents, we have all felt that sick, empty, queasy feeling in our stomach, dryness in the throat, and the gentle sting of tears forming in our eyes when we hear of a tragic story of someone losing a young child. This is especially true when it happens to a family member, friend, or close acquaintance. Most say they cannot imagine having to go through that.

This tragedy happened to our family January 1, 2007, with the accidental drowning of our son William (Lil' Bill) M. Gough III at the tender age of 23.

There have been many blessings that have come from Bill's death. I do not have room to share them all here, but I will talk about a couple. First, we were all together as a family on vacation in Palm Springs, California, during Bill's Christmas break from Auburn University. We know exactly how Bill died, and we were with him at the pool when he passed out from a heart arrhythmia due to complications from diabetes. Next, the reaction from friends and family was tremendous, including a group of insurance agency owners sending me a check to do something in Bill's memory. I took that check and started the William Gough III Charitable Memorial Fund for the first of several scholarships that have now been permanently endowed. Later, I founded BGI Marketing Systems designed to help insurance agency owners that believed investing in my selling systems and processes could take their business to another level. A portion of every dollar that comes in to BGI is donated to the William Gough III Charitable Memorial Fund. You can read more about BGI and Bill's story at www.BGIMarketing.com.

I missed a lot in 2007, went to some dark places, and stayed out of the office three to four months. Amazingly, the staff was motivated to succeed, and we had the best year in our history at that time. One of the most rewarding things that year was I personally awarded Bill's first memorial scholarship to a lady my age who told me if not for that $1,000.00 gift she could not attend school.

The following section on our referral rewards program describes how we started our charity giving in 2006, the year prior to Bill's passing. I believe there are no coincidences for this occurrence.

Bill Gough All American Insurance Agency Referral Program

Before being exposed to direct-response marketing in late 2004, we were pathetic at generating referrals in my insurance agency. Referrals were generating only 2% to 3% of our new business sales. Even though our industry is strongly regulated by state insurance departments, I could give a small reward for referral as long as it was not based on a sales transaction. In other words, I could give a small gift card, lottery ticket, etc., as a referral reward as long as it wasn't tied to a sale. If we quoted ten referrals and wrote five of them, we had to reward all ten, not just the five that purchased insurance.

In 2005, after more than 20 years in business, we decided to make a major effort to drive referrals in our insurance agency. We also discovered we could add a monthly random drawing of the month's referrers and an end-of-year grand prize to make the referral program even more attractive. We immediately went to work hard on this as a company and made sure we announced this to our customers, prospects, and centers of influence. This was done in many ways and used different media. It was a slow process, but gained momentum fast as we continued to talk strategy in our office meetings. In other words, we decided our business was going to be about referrals, and we would constantly keep it at the forefront of the business. Everyone in the agency had a role in this critical part of our business. We put together a ruthless measurement and accountability system in the referral process.

Our measurable results were amazing: In 2005 our new business from referrals went from a paltry 3% to a very respectable 17% of our new business sales. In 2006, we added charity giving to the program and got a big bump in response. Referrals were 23% of new business sales, and we raised money for four charities. From 2007–2009 we had a separate referral reward program just for realtors and mortgage lenders. Today, 34% of our new business auto and homeowner sales comes from referrals.

Some of the marketing and media we used to promote the referral program include:

1. Referral fliers and everything else revolved around the program fliers that were on all desks, mailed out in every outgoing piece of mail. (See Figures 13.1A and B on pages 134 and 135.)

2. Dedicated a full page in our printed monthly newsletter with contest details and, very importantly, recognized our customers for their referrals, plus a photo of the monthly winner with a staff member.

3. Weekly emails to our realtor mortgage broker lists with photo of current monthly winner and previous year grand prize winners . . . this weekly email also gives a valuable business tip each week.

4. Referral program on all employee auto-signatures for their outgoing emails.

5. Monthly email to customers and prospects recognizing our monthly winner and all referrers for the previous month and, of course, the details of the program for all to participate.

6. Personal URL website sent to customers through email with link to give referrals.

7. Directed customers to use custom tabs on agency Facebook to submit referrals.

8. Fax cover sheets were created with referral rewards program on the bottom.

9. Special referral-only mail pieces were created . . . both postcards and letters.

10. Handwritten thank-you notes to the referrers mailed immediately upon the referral.

11. Measurement was key. We hold staff and each other strictly accountable. Check out the detail of my measurements below for first six years of referral program.

The results of our referral program January 2005–December 2010:

- 1,720 home and/or auto insurance leads received just from referrals

- 1,027 new auto and/or homeowners insurance policies written
- 59.71% closing ratio on these referred leads
- $715,362.85 new home and/or auto insurance premiums written for referrals
- 99% preferred home and auto policies, highest lifetime value
- 93.37% retention on these 1,027 policies
- $223,301.70 new business, renewal, and bonus commissions
- $31,890.70 referral campaign total expenses
- 7.02 to 1 return on investment . . . increases yearly (expenses are in first year only)

> **DAN KENNEDY'S COMMENT**: Figures 13.1A and B are two pages from Bill's insurance agency's customer newsletter, all about the referral program. I think it's important to understand that the big-brand company Allstate would be extremely unlikely to run a promotional program like this or send out a homemade-looking, personal newsletter, but when done by Bill building his agency brand it works well. And having Allstate as his product brand makes all his marketing more powerful. You should also carefully examine the list of the 11 things he's doing to fuel his referral program. *Eleven*. Most business owners announce a referral reward opportunity, put up an in-store sign, maybe put out a flier, then wonder why it doesn't produce. The principle here is that EVERYTHING needs to be aggressively marketed—brand(s), product(s), service(s), referral program(s).

FIGURE 13.1A: Referral Flier, Front

OUT OF THIS WORLD REFERRAL PROGRAM

Bill Gough's All—American Agency Is Shooting For The Moon!

Help us skyrocket our referrals of clients, friends, co-workers, and acquaintances - as long as they contact the office for a FREE, NO OBLIGATION quote YOU WIN:

Wow!

- $10.00 Gift Card for each referral
- $10.00 donation made on your behalf to the Bill Gough III Scholarship
- Entry to win MONTHLY $50.00 Gift Card
- Entry to win GRAND PRIZE LED TV to be given away December 2011!

THIS COULD BE

Remember, the person you refer does **NOT** have to become our client for you to win!

Bill Just Got Back From The Moon!

2010 GRAND PRIZE WINNER

VP of Agency Operations Wendy Murphy with Rhonda Webster from Huntsville, Alabama. Rhonda was our grand prize winner of a Flat Screen TV just for telling her friends and clients about the Bill Gough All American Insurance

Contact Bill Gough's All American Agency!!

Mail: 321 S Walnut St, Florence, AL 35630 **E-Mail:** WendyMurphy@Allstate.com
Phone: 256-765-2200 or Toll Free: 888-765-2201 **Fax:** 256-765-2201
Website: www.QuoteMeBill.com

FIGURE 13.1B: Referral Flier, Back

BILL GOUGH III MEMORIAL SCHOLARSHIP

Bill Gough III
9/20/1983 – 1/1/2007

In 2010 YOUR REFERRALS raised $3,620.00. We started this Fund in April of 2007 and since then we have received a total of $26,685.00 in contributions.

Your referrals play a big part in Lil' Bill's fund... each time you tell someone about our office and they call for a quote, we donate $10.00 on your behalf. No purchase necessary on their part. *Refer yourself and we'll do the same for you!*

In 2010, Vanessa & Bill Gough awarded the 2010-2011 Bill Gough III Scholarship to Brandy Wilson

Bill Gough & Scholarship Recipient Brandy Wilson

Provides First Class Service – Goes the Extra Mile!

GET A LOOK AT WHAT WE'RE DOING!

"As a REALTOR, I get asked all the time who I recommend for this or that. When my clients ask me to refer them to someone for any type of service, I understand that it can be a direct reflection on myself. Bill Gough and his staff have not only provided **FIRST CLASS** service to everyone I have sent their way, but they have always gone the extra mile to meet the needs of each individual client and situation.

They impress me time and time again. In fact, they now handle all of my personal insurance needs as well. And the best part, they saved me money too - icing on the cake!"

Mike Randall, Realtor with Coldwell Banker, Florence, AL

2010 $50.00 Gift Card Winners

Roxanne Benefield, Florence, AL   Chip Grinkmeyer, Birmingham, AL
Brad Flippo, Florence, AL   Pat Burney, Florence, AL
Lynn Francis, Florence, AL   Mike Randall, Florence, AL
Charles & Helen Staggs, Waterloo, AL   Rhonda Webster, Huntsville. AL
Margaret Keeton, Tuscumbia, AL   Tammy Gordon, Rogersville, AL

Contact Bill Gough's
All American Agency!
Mail: 321 S Walnut St, Florence, AL 35630
E-Mail: WendyMurphy@allstate.com
Phone: 256-765-2200 or Toll Free 888-765-2201 **Fax:** 256-765-2201
Website: www.QuoteMeBill.com

Bill Gough
President, BGAAA

Wendy Murphy
VP Operations

The Power of a
Printed Monthly Newsletter

Dan Kennedy says it best, *"Done right, the monthly printed newsletter is the most powerful relationship-building tool for small-business owners and entrepreneurs."*

I was first introduced to the concept of the printed monthly newsletter in early 2005 and really liked the appeal of it. I put it on the "to-do list," and it kept getting pushed back as I never realized the difficulty of this task because I had never done anything like it before. Finally, after more than a year we launched it in April 2006, and it became an immediate hit with our customers. I am very proud of our production team, as we have only missed publishing it one month, just after Bill's death in 2007.

The newsletter works best if done similar to Aunt Betty's Christmas letter telling the stories of her family over the past year. It is a feel-good publication providing helpful, useful information designed to improve your customers' lives. It gets into the home working for you, and has good shelf life provided you are interesting and not being a sales pest—or even worse, boring.

It also serves as a customer magnet attracting more cross-sells and upsells from your customers. Referrals will skyrocket with a well-promoted referral rewards program. Customer retention improves as you build trust and loyalty with your raving customer fans. You will become the expert in your marketplace and dominate your competition because they have no idea of this incredible relationship-marketing tool.

A couple of questions about newsletters I always get are: 1) Why monthly? Is quarterly enough? 2) Can I just do an e-newsletter?

Of course you can easily say yes to both of these, but I strongly suggest not.

Today we are bombarded with thousands of messages daily, and people are busier than ever. This reason alone should be enough to want your valuable message in the home or business of your customers every 30 days. A peer of mine tested dropping his monthly newsletter to a quarterly publication and after just six months went back to monthly. His referrals really dropped off, and many of his customers complained about not receiving their beloved publication. His test proved it for me.

An enewsletter is cheap, sure, but it is so much harder to consume a large amount of information. If you insist on doing an enewsletter, do it, but also do the printed version. The printed newsletter is the best way to build valuable relationships. Try sending your mother an e-birthday card and see how that goes for you.

Here is an example of a cover story for my newsletter, featuring a story of my wife and daughter Bailey's experience with an auto accident. (See Figure 13.2 on page 138.) The story includes a picture of Vanessa and Bailey with the damaged SUV that hooks the reader. I then pivot to ". . . if you happen to be involved in an auto accident here are the five things you must do." I could easily have written an article about those five things as laid out on home office boring brochures. Vanessa's story is real with photo as proof and demonstrates how accidents can happen to anyone. No faceless corporation or clever caveman ad can compete with these real world experiences in my customer newsletter each month.

We also have a done-for-you newsletter program for insurance agency owners. More info at www.bgimarketing.com.

FIGURE 13.2: Newsletter Cover Story

September 2007   *News and Tips to Make Your Life Easier, Safer, and Happier...*

Circle of Safety
For Friends & Clients of the All American Agency

Bill Gough
President & Agency Owner

Inside
This Issue

Bill Gough All American
Insurance Agency

Representing Allstate
Insurance Company

321 S Walnut St
Florence, AL 35630
(256) 765-2200
(888) 765-2201

Now serving the states of
AL, TN, GA and MS!

The Backyard Trampoline
Meet Me in the Emergency Room

At a summer birthday party this month, I was reminded how dangerous backyard trampolines really are.

No, nobody got hurt. The trampoline was in full swing with four and five kids at a time having a ball (some of them mine).

Meanwhile I was chatting with a friend who's a nurse at ECM Hospital in Florence. She rattled off all the serious injuries she has seen personally in the Emergency Room. It unnerved me.

Now, if you ever watched kids play on a trampoline, you know this much: They jump around in groups. Nobody "spots" them for the irresistible somersault attempts and back-flips. And parents are nowhere in sight.

The reason I bring this up is simple: Backyard trampolines are popping up everywhere. Kids love them, especially "the neighborhood kids." And a backyard trampoline is a quick and easy way to have your homeowner policy non-renewed or declined.

The standard insurance industry application for coverage now specifically asks, *"Is there a trampoline on the premises?"* This wasn't true only a few years ago.

Insurance companies want to know for the obvious reason: trampoline injuries result in expensive personal injury lawsuits. The trampolines work just fine, it's the homeowner, though, who fails to supervise and take the prudent steps to insure safety.

After the party, I did some research. Trampoline injuries

(Continued on page 3)

Life Lessons Learned the Hard Way

Vanessa, Bailey (back), Taylor (front)

It was a beautiful Thursday morning – the sun shining, the birds chirping – and I'm enjoying a beautiful view of the lake from my office window at home.

I just finished pouring a fresh cup of coffee and was listening to a business conference call when my wife, Vanessa, passed by my office doors on her way to go workout. At this point, I was intently listening to my call and barely saw her wave goodbye as she passed. Feeling a bit guilty, I rushed to the garage and gave her a kiss goodbye.

6 minutes later, my cell rings…it was Vanessa. "Now wait a minute, she knows I'm on an important call," I thought to myself. I answered and her panicky tone immediately told me something was wrong…

(Continued on page 2)

DAN KENNEDY'S COMMENT: Bill's choice is a vital one. There are two ways to present useful information like "The 5 Things To Do If Involved In A Car Accident": his way or in a simple, straightforward, factual, and instructional way, as most big companies would do, probably in a marketing piece plastered with corporate logo. That has two chief drawbacks. One, any company can do the very same thing. It is generic information. Two, maybe more importantly, it's boring. I teach that the ultimate marketing sin is being boring. So Bill's way, engaging the consumer/reader with a first-person, personal story, then gradually segueing to the instructional information, serves to make it proprietary and interesting. Fortunately, there is no law that dictates, if you have a brand, or operate under the umbrella of a brand, you must make it the focal point of everything you do.

Author a Book

If the customer newsletter is the most powerful relationship-building tool, your book is the ultimate positioning tool that elevates you miles above your competition.

A couple of books I authored and used in my insurance agency were written for a specific audience for a very specific purpose. My first book, *A Business Success Journal,* which I co-authored, was written for business owners to help launch and grow my referral rewards program. I made this book readily available as gifts to my commercial insurance business owner customers and my COI businesses.

My main COIs are mortgage brokers, realtors, and various dealerships selling automobiles, boats, mobile homes, and motorcycles. All of these businesses have weekly meetings. I would just call and get on the agenda for five to ten minutes, give them some helpful info about how we could serve them, and gift them my book. The "Wow" factor of the book was the unique positioning I had over every competitor in the marketplace. I must be an expert, right? I wrote this book on success, and I'm offering to serve them with helpful information that can help their business with a little implementation.

My next book I authored and published myself, *Informed and Insured: Everything You Need To Know About Insurance Before You Pay Your Next Premium.* It was written for anyone that needs personal insurance, including auto, home, life, and personal recreational vehicles. The purpose of the book is to provide very helpful information for buying personal lines of insurance. It strongly suggests avoiding the huge mistake of self-service by trying to buy insurance online and from the 1-800 numbers.

Informed and Insured suggests using a trusted insurance advisor, not a policy peddler, and who better to help than an author of the book on how to successfully buy personal lines of insurance.

A book makes a very powerful offer for your direct-response advertising and marketing. We

---

RESOURCES

If you are in the insurance industry, you should definitely check out the book and newsletter publishing programs Bill provides, at www.BGIMarketing.com. Whatever business or profession you're in, if your interest is piqued about being the author of a book get a copy of the book, *Book The Business: How To Make Big Money With Your Book Without Even Selling A Single Copy* by Dan Kennedy and Adam Witty, from Amazon.com, BN.com, any bookseller, or advantagefamily.com. And you can find resources for customer newsletter publishing at DanKennedy.com/store.

FIGURE 13.3: Book Covers

use it constantly in print media, direct mail, email marketing, social media, customer newsletter, and live radio ads.

Authorship may seem like a Herculean task. It sure did to me when I first thought of the idea. Basically, I just wrote out the information I constantly share with my customers, prospects, and COIs. I'm not saying it's easy, because it is not, but getting your content on paper that you deliver on a regular basis is not that difficult. If you are an insurance agency owner or work in an agency, you may qualify to buy the authorship rights to *Informed and Insured.* You can refer to our website for more information.

Above are the covers of my two books written for two very different audiences, one for business owners and one for the personal lines insurance buying public. (See Figure 13.3.) Both of these books serve my business well.

Free-Standing Newspaper Insert

One of the best ways to really stand out in your local market is the use of newspaper inserts. Most newspapers allow you to target certain ZIP codes if you wish, and in my experience the rates are much better than regular newspaper ads.

Figures 13.4A and 13.4B on pages 143 and 144 are great examples of one of my BGI Elite Mastermind Members using a direct-response ad with a great offer on the front and leveraging the power of the Allstate Insurance Brand on the back. Allstate will even pay for half of this ad because it is one of their co-op approved advertisements.

> **DAN KENNEDY'S COMMENT**: One side of this FSI uses an ad created and provided by Allstate, and, frankly, it is fairly typical corporate brand advertising. I judge it mediocre and ordinary at best. But combined with the other side that Jason created, a great direct-response ad with all the right direct-response elements*, he gets the best of both worlds: the umbrella of the known and trusted Allstate brand, the effectiveness of direct response. This is a terrific example of marrying brand and DR. (*The elements used here are benefit-driven headline; breaking news [first paragraph]; guarantee; testimonials; offer with deadline.)

Like All Marriages, There's Give 'n Take and Tension

The marriages of a big, corporate brand and a local business brand with aggressive direct-response marketing hasn't been a simple or easy one. It has its times and places of conflict. They don't go together like peas in a pod. As you can hopefully

FIGURE 13.4A: Direct-Response Ad, Front

ATTN: New York Residents...

"Our NEW Rates are So Low...

I Guarantee to Save You AT LEAST $307⁰⁰ Per Year on Your Auto and Home Insurance or I'll Pay You $20⁰⁰!"

"Jason helped us SAVE $842.00 per year on our auto and home insurance when we switched from Geico and Liberty Mutual to The Jason Juliano Agency! Plus, he simplified our 3 policies into 2, got us a low monthly payment, and increased all our coverages for a lot less money!"
-Jeffrey Greene
Rochester, NY

"Jason helped me save almost $30.00 per month ($360.00 per year!) on my auto, home, and motorcycle insurance switching from State Farm to The Jason Juliano Agency! He even upgraded all of our coverages for less money. No other agent we've ever had has taken the time to explain what each coverage means and why the coverage is so important!"
-Rick Dunn
Batavia, NY

Dear Friend,

The auto & home insurance carriers I work with **just LOWERED RATES in NY state**! We've been helping your neighbors in save hundreds of dollars per year.

In fact, I'm so confident I can save you money - I even guarantee to save you at least $307.00 per year when you get a home and auto insurance quote. If I can't save you $307.00 - I'll pay you $20.00 as my penalty just for wasting your time. *(You just need to qualify for auto and home insurance.)*

ONE CALL DOES IT ALL! We'll cancel your existing policies for you, request any refund you may be owed, PLUS notify DMV, your bank, and contact your mortgage company for escrow payment, making the process easy and pain-free for you!!

Pick up the phone and call me at **(585) 344-1400.** When you call, be sure to ask for a copy of my special report: **"9 Secrets to Saving on Auto & Home Insurance that the Big Insurance Companies Don't Want You to Know About!"** yours FREE regardless if we do business or not.

Plus! Have a conversation with me about your home and auto insurance by July 31st and receive an entry into the drawing for a **FREE 42" LCD TV** - no purchase necessary. There's no pressure or obligation to buy anything!

Call (585) 344-1400 Right Now!

To Take Advantage of These Incredibly Low Rates You MUST Qualify:
☑ No Major Claims/Accidents
☑ No Major Violations
☑ Above Average Credit History
☑ Currently Have Insurance

"We saved over $40.00 per month when we switched – that's almost $500.00 per year in savings! Our auto and home insurance costs are SO LOW with The Jason Juliano Agency that we would never switch away! We left State Farm after we got married, Jason called us to tell us about NEW DISCOUNTS we qualified for! How often does your insurance agent call to reduce your already low prices?"
-Todd Perkins
Rochester, NY

"I was with NY Central paying $100.00 per month... I came over to The Jason Juliano Agency and am now paying less than $80.00 per month. ($240 per year in savings!) They take care of me in a professional and prompt manner and I'm very happy with the service they give me!" **-Annika Kohler** - LeRoy, NY

*"Sloan and I have been **completely satisfied** with your service. You have offered solutions and changes to our policies that have increased our coverages and saved us money. Our new improved auto policy has superior coverage and we still saved an additional $438 per year!"*
-Mike & Sloan Lechner - Pavilion, NY

FREE $10 Gift Card

Bring this flyer into my office WITH your current auto and home insurance policies, and receive a $10.00 gift card to a local restaurant, store, or gas card. No purchase necessary. No pressure or obligation to buy anything! Go to 590 East Main St (across from Aldi's) in Batavia. (585) 344-1400. Expires 12/31/2013

590 East Main Street
Batavia, NY 14020
(across from Aldi's)
Jason@JulianoAgency.com

FIGURE 13.4B: Direct-Response Ad, Back

Your roof could help reduce your rate.
When your new roof goes up, your premium could go down. If you recently purchased a new home or replaced the roof on your current home, with Allstate House & Home Insurance you may qualify for a lower rate. Call me today for a free quote.

JASON JULIANO
585-344-1400
590 EAST MAIN STREET
BATAVIA
jasonjuliano@allstate.com

Allstate.
You're in good hands.

Auto   Home   Life   Retirement

see from the results I've shared here, it's definitely worth the trouble! I can say with rock-solid certainty that I would not have reached the pinnacle of success within the Allstate agency community if I had simply relied on the power of the Allstate brand and their advertising to carry me. I can assure you, I would not have made as good an income or created as much equity in my agency if I hadn't built my own, local brand, The All-American Agency, as well as my personal brand. As I've explained, I would never have achieved anything close to what I have by depending on brand and image marketing. Injecting direct-response advertising into both the upfront attraction of new clients and the back-end retention of clients and mobilizing my referral armies was the rocket fuel.

BILL GOUGH built one of the most successful Allstate Insurance agencies in America, and provides training, coaching, and marketing support to more than 1,000 Allstate agency owners as well as other insurance brokers, agents, and professionals through his BGI Marketing organization, www. BGIMarketing.com.

CHAPTER 14

How to Meld Mass Media and Direct Media

by Nick Nanton and J.W. Dicks,
Celebrity Branding Agency

To set out to create and build a brand, to make a brand meaningful and valuable, or to leverage and profit from an established brand—whether one that is personal, corporate, or attached to a product either local or global—you must gain access to media and know how to use it to your advantage.

Imagine a new movie studio starting up with modest means. Anxious to get off on the right foot, they put every dollar into making the most amazing feature film anyone has ever seen.

Note two critical words in that last sentence: "every dollar." Because when the studio finishes this amazing movie, they have no money left to market it. They can't get anyone to see it because they don't have any funds to tell anyone about it.

Anxious not to repeat that mistake, they raise more money and put a bundle into hiring the best movie marketing company in the country to sell their next very modestly budgeted film. The marketing company delivers to them an incredibly impactful film trailer and a series of exciting TV commercials that make this movie feel like a "Have to See" event.

Except, again, they've spent everything. Now they have no money to do any publicity—which means they can't afford to get the movie's stars to do the critical media events— such as the all-important press junkets and appearances on entertainment news shows and late-night talk shows—that establish awareness and credibility for the film. They also don't have the funds to hold screenings for important media critics, create press releases that talk about the film's unique qualities, or create a killer social media presence that could drive the movie into blockbuster territory. All they have is a bunch of commercials that people may or may not see.

The moral of this story?

Simple. There is no one success ingredient that can stand alone. Even a studio with a great brand, say Disney, can make two films—each with its own brand, say, *Iron Man* and *The Lone Ranger*—and get two very different outcomes. Brand is no assurance of success. We believe there are three critical success factors that must be given: attention, energy, and investment. We call this the Business Trifecta. If you wager on the Trifecta at a racetrack—Dan Kennedy's second home—you have to get all three of the top-finishing horses, first, second, and third, on the same ticket from a single bet, and if you do, you usually get a big payoff. But two out of three pays zero. As does one out of three.

The fact is that you can't properly build your brand or grow your business without employing what we call the Business Trifecta—the unbeatable combination of media, marketing, and PR that creates visibility, establishes credibility, and effectively sells who you are and what you do. If you're missing any component of that trifecta—well, it's kind of like trying to sit on a three-legged stool with one leg missing. At some point, you're going to wind up on the floor!

At the Dicks + Nanton Celebrity Branding Agency, we're very strong believers in using storytelling—or what we call "StorySelling™"—to really build your branding power. We've seen the amazing results it brings. But those results only come from using the Business Trifecta to tell your brand story in the proper way and with the necessary impact.

To better understand how the Business Trifecta combines to powerfully StorySell™, we should first talk about each of its "legs"—and what each of them contributes to the trifecta. We'll start, naturally, with the first leg . . .

Successful Use of MEDIA

Most entrepreneurs and professionals create their own media to tell their own story—or they use an outside agency such as ours to do the job for them. That media can be in the form of a branded film, a book, an audio CD, a special report, and so forth.

This kind of media is usually not a client's main business, even though media can be sold just like any informational product. For instance, a tax specialist could write a book on tax secrets. That book could then be sold on Amazon, even though the specialist's main business is, obviously, helping his or her own clients with their tax issues. The book serves as an indirect advertisement for the specialist, who positions himself as an expert in how to pay the least amount of taxes possible.

Of course, it's sometimes more worthwhile to give the media away for free to generate leads, establish expertise, and grab contact info for future marketing. Downloadable information on company websites that require an email entry for access to that kind of media is a prime example.

We also place our clients in such nationally recognized media outlets as CBS, ABC, and NBC TV affiliates, *The Wall Street Journal, Forbes,* etc. These kinds of "Big Media" appearances are enormously important to establishing credibility; not everybody shows up in *USA Today,* after all!

There is a strong afterglow to these kinds of media appearances and mentions. The "As Seen On" and "As Seen In" credits have life long after the day of the paragraph's publication or the minutes of air time occurred. We have a system for guaranteeing our clients these media appearances and mentions, to get these credits, and usually to get them in a hurry. It is certainly possible, though, to make their pursuit a do-it-yourself proposition. Because media appearances tend to create more media interest, a snowball effect can occur.

Whatever media you choose to work with, it's important, from our viewpoint, to always provide some kind of value to the viewer/reader/listener. You should either be providing valuable information or just telling a great story about yourself and your business that people will love to hear. Whatever your creative approach, the presentation of the media and the packaging can be the first step in establishing the critical elements of credibility and trust. It doesn't have to be a high-class Hollywood production, but it does have to feel authentic and demonstrate your expertise.

But no matter how good your media is, you also need . . .

Successful Use of PR

Let's say your media efforts go so well that you end up being interviewed on a popular national show, such as *Good Morning America*. Well, even though you've made an amazing media breakthrough with that appearance, to most people out there you're just a five-minute segment that goes by and disappears forever . . . unless you use PR to keep the excitement humming.

PR, or public relations, is all about creating *awareness*. You know the age-old question: If a tree falls in a forest and nobody's around, does it make a sound? Well, PR doesn't really care about the answer to that question—it just wants to make sure somebody *is* around to hear when that tree hits the ground.

There are basically two types of PR—pre-PR and post-PR. Pre-PR is the classic form of public relations, when you announce something that is about to happen and hope that you get coverage and attention. For example, you might want to promote the fact that you're going to be on *Good Morning America*. Or that you're about to open another office location, made a major hire, or are expanding your products or services into new territory. It could be a personal achievement, such as receiving an honorary doctorate or being honored as "Business of the Year" at the local Rotary Club. Whatever the topic, it should be something that justifies a press release and, at the same time, keeps your brand top-of-the-mind with your public.

Post-PR is what you do after something happens. Let's go back to that *Good Morning America* interview; even though it may have been over in a few minutes, you can make it last forever with post-PR by putting out a press release about the interview, sharing some of the content, and, in the online press release, including a link to a clip of the interview on the network website, YouTube, or wherever it happens to land.

PR exists to amplify your StorySelling™. Let's say your company just sold its one millionth widget—why not announce that fact? It shows your business is very established and very successful. Press releases boost awareness and continue to build positive word-of-mouth about your company. And, if that press release hits the right place at the right time, it could land you a story in the newspaper, in a magazine, on a local radio or TV station, or on an online site—even a national one. It can also get you invited on radio and TV interview shows to talk about that special millionth widget.

Most importantly, online press releases, the kind we like to focus on, show up heavily in search engine results. So, if potential customers or clients Google your name or the name of your company, the first impression they'll get is going to be a favorable one. Instead of just coming up with your website or your LinkedIn profile, you'll have people reacting by saying, "Hey—this guy sold a million of his widgets and was on *Good Morning America*—he's the real deal!" Online press releases significantly boost your internet presence and, because they're written in the third person, also act as powerful online testimonials to anyone Googling you or your business. They appear to be a normal news story to the average reader.

The right PR could nab you special media appearances, lead to other news stories, and drive more traffic to your website. The main cost comes from hiring a PR company to help you make all of that happen. But, unless you have a legitimate story that really *does* stand out, that PR firm might be hard-pressed to get you much of an afterlife beyond that initial press release.

As a matter of fact, that's one of the biggest mistakes we see companies make—hiring PR firms when they don't have the marketing or media to back it up. When you try to get PR without a story big enough to catch people's attention . . . well, let's get back to that tree falling in the forest fable. In this case, there *are* people around to hear it—but nobody really bothers to listen. That's why, again, we swear by the Business Trifecta.

But hang on for more about how that works . . . after we explain the third and final member of that trio . . .

Successful Use of MARKETING

Marketing, of course, is how you drive revenue for your brand. It's how you actually promote your products and/or services to your public.

And let's spend a moment and talk about that public. Have you taken the time to actually narrow down your main niche when it comes to your most likely customers? It's always the most cost-effective if you can zoom in on a small group that is most disposed to clamor for what you're selling. You can truly mine "riches from niches"—because you can market more aggressively, more often, and more effectively to a smaller and more receptive crowd.

Many marketers often make the big mistake of trying to sell to too many people at once—which rapidly drains your marketing budget. At the same time, you don't realize as much revenue from your marketing because you're trying to sell to a lot of people who probably don't want what you're offering in the first place. That's why, especially when you're starting out, you want to determine your best target group for marketing and focus your efforts on them.

It is also easier to achieve brand recognition in a small pond than a large ocean, particularly when you and the brand you're trying to build has great relevance and significance to the particular fish in that pond. Dan Kennedy calls this Message-to-Market Match, and it links to Brand-to-Market Match.

The purpose of your marketing, of course, can be multi-faceted. You may want to drive people to your website . . . and then, have your website convince them to leave their contact info . . . and then, generate an email sequence designed to get them to buy. Or you may want a simple, targeted campaign with just one end result in mind—a simple sales letter designed to get people to buy your product, for example.

As this entire book advises and demonstrates, the use of direct-response advertising and marketing is the clearer, cleaner, shorter path to revenue than other approaches, and it can build your brand right along with generating leads, converting them to customers, and putting money in the bank.

With any approach, it's always hard to make a sale "cold"—without having already established yourself with the prospect in question. Which is why we believe you need to employ . . .

A Fully Integrated Approach

If you examine the art of storytelling, you'll find that stories don't work without a setup. You need to know the people involved, their situation, and whatever challenge they have to face. That setup could be as short as a line in a simple joke ("A guy walks into a bar . . .)—or as long as a few hundred pages in the beginning of an old Russian novel. But unless you *understand* what the story is about, unless the setup *explains* the basic facts to you, the plot, and most importantly, the ending won't make any sense. Imagine only seeing the last 20 minutes of *Star Wars*—"Wait, what was that Death Star thing? Who's that girl with the weird hair?"—you'd think you saw some cool special effects but would have no idea why any of them mattered.

Sales are the end game to your brand and your business, which is why most entrepreneurs emphasize marketing so much; to them, that's the quickest way to those all-important sales and ongoing success.

BUT . . . unless you prepare your audience and unless you give them the crucial "setup" beforehand, it's going to be hard to make those sales happen. Unless they know who you are and trust in what you do and sell, they're not likely to give you their credit card numbers.

It's why chain stores and restaurants tend to do so well; customers know what to expect from them and understand that a certain standard of quality is in place. The setup has already been provided by their mass marketing, as well as the public's previous experience patronizing their various locations.

You, however, don't have the instant recognition and trust that a Home Depot or a Walmart triggers with a glance at their logo. That's why the Business Trifecta is so important to implement—because it's designed to do the setup that provides recognition and trust *before* you make a direct sales pitch.

Here's how it works.

The Business Trifecta begins with creating effective **media,** as we've discussed. One of the ways we do that for our clients is by producing a great, high-quality hardcover book that's got an attractive, eye-catching cover, powerful overall theme, and the participation of a lot of great authors. Those authors usually only have to worry about contributing a chapter rather than generating an entire book—making it much easier on their end. They still get credit for authoring the book, however, and can order special customized copies of the book with their picture on the cover. Still another way is to create a polished branded film that uses StorySelling™ to focus on a business, entrepreneur, or professional. By structuring the content of the film correctly and telling the right story, you can create a movie that people will respond to on a positive and emotional level.

Whatever media is decided upon (and, obviously, a multimedia approach can be incredibly effective), it should have a high impact factor. For example, we ensure that our books are bestsellers and our branded films have high production values.

Because the created media does have that high impact factor, we can move on to the next member of our Trifecta—**PR.** High-profile media makes a great story for PR. Participation in one of our books, for example, means you can benefit from the pre-PR and post-PR we discussed earlier. For example, one press release would focus on you signing with our publishing arm for a book deal and another one would announce that your book reached bestseller status. You can also obviously do PR about a branded film being released (you can even host a premiere of the film at a local theater).

The real value of PR is that it makes your media live forever. Your press releases stay online and continue to show up in Google results—even though your media may have been released months or even years ago.

Which brings us back to our third member of the Trifecta—**marketing.** Because you have the media in place and you've done the PR about the media, you've generated a lot of substantial "setup" about you and your business—and you can now use that setup to finish your StorySelling™ and actually pitch your products and services. Your PR and media efforts are already there to establish your credibility and visibility. Not many people have written books or starred in movies. That's impressive, and it says something about who you are and what your level of expertise is.

And it gives you a much better shot at convincing someone to buy from you.

Let's face it. It's easier now than at any time to market, thanks to the internet. That's why, more than at any other time, we all need to find a way to differentiate ourselves from the rest of the pack.

The Business Trifecta does just that.

Media feeds into PR, which feeds into marketing. All three components create a powerful machine that ends up driving more and more revenue. Each makes the other more effective than it otherwise would have been.

Which brings us to the magic ingredient of our special formula . . .

Melding Media

What we left out of our discussion of media earlier in this chapter is the fact that there are *two kinds of media.*

Mass media is the type most people know about. We're talking about commercial TV networks, national magazines, radio stations, etc. that are operated specifically to bring in consumers of all stripes. Mass media is about numbers—they want to attract the most users, so they can't really mess around. They *must* produce content that's genuine and interesting to the most people or they lose money.

All of us put the "mass" into mass media—we seek it out every day by watching our favorite shows, reading our favorite newspapers, listening to our favorite music, and so forth. And because it has no other visible agenda than to entertain and inform the most people, mass media automatically brings two things to the table—awareness and credibility. If there's a story about you on *CNN,* people 1) see it and 2) think more of you because of it. (Unless, of course, you just murdered somebody or something, but we won't get into that here!)

This is why people hire PR companies—to get them on mass media outlets. The problem is, you can't "eat" awareness and credibility—in other words, if there isn't a direct solicitation involved with a mass media appearance, it's not really a big revenue generator. And chances are, if you did score an interview with *Good Morning America,* they're not going to let you sell your stuff while you're sitting there chatting it up with the host.

Now, let's talk about the second kind of media, known as "direct media." Most of you have created something in this arena—it's a targeted informational sales tool that takes the form of a CD, DVD, newsletter, direct-mail piece, website copy, etc. The business distributes this direct media to an audience it selects (or in most cases the audience has identified itself by "opting in" on its website) with the sole purpose of selling to that audience—and it's created by that business for that specific purpose.

The problem? As we've already hinted at, *direct media lacks credibility.* There's a reason direct-mail campaigns only have an average response rate of from a fraction of 1% to no more than 3%. Whenever anyone knows that a business is directly trying to sell to them, they immediately put up their guard and get suspicious. They don't know if what the sales piece is telling them is true because they know that the company is mainly interested in their money.

One way around this credibility gap is to use testimonials, product reviews, and other third-party verification that appears objective. But there's still another way around it that works just as well, if not better . . . and that's melding *both* kinds of media—mass media and direct media—into one.

Go to our website at www.celebritybrandingagency.com. You'll see, near the top of the home page, "AS SEEN IN . . ." followed by a line of instantly recognizable logos of leading media outlets. We don't put those logos there to brag and be obnoxious—we do it because it's a vital part of our marketing philosophy. When someone comes to check out our website, we want them to see that powerful lineup—and to immediately understand that we're established professionals who work with some of the biggest media companies in the world.

And we want our clients to have the same advantage— which is why we advocate placing them in such publications as *USA Today* or on such networks as CNN. When you can talk about those kinds of mass media appearances in your direct media, that direct media suddenly has an awesome level of credibility it would otherwise be lacking. If someone sees national media logos on your direct-mail marketing piece, again, you're suddenly elevated in their eyes to a national expert (which you may already be—but might have a hard time convincing a stranger of that fact).

Whenever you're able to be a part of the mass media conversation, you should always leverage it to your maximum marketing advantage. Say you managed to get a spot on CNBC talking about your business. You trumpet that fact on your website, your newsletter, your e-zine, whatever direct media piece you create. That mass media "stamp of approval" can mean the world to a potential customer.

Even better is if you post a copy of that appearance on your website, or put a copy of your newspaper article into a direct-mail piece. We even hang ours up on our office walls— and our clients will invariably comment on them, which inevitably leads to us telling those clients how they can get the same coverage for themselves.

So ask yourself—don't you think that kind of mass media "stamp of approval" will get you taken a little bit more seriously? We can tell you, based on literally hundreds of case studies, it absolutely will get people to pay closer attention to you and what you have to offer.

So get yourself some mass media credibility—and insert it into your direct media. Don't spend all your time and money trying to get on TV or in the paper without having a plan for using that mass media exposure in conjunction with direct media for your marketing.

When you successfully combine media, marketing, and PR, you guarantee yourself business growth and increased revenues. Correctly using the Business Trifecta raises your enterprise to the next level—and trust us, you'll enjoy the view from up there!

NICK NANTON and **J.W. DICKS** lead The Celebrity Branding Agency®. Nick is an Emmy-winning documentary film director and producer, a gifted and skilled business storyteller, and an exceptionally knowledgeable media insider. J.W. Dicks is a strategic business development advisor and a securities and franchise attorney. They have perfected systems for personal and business credits. They are also the authors of *Celebrity Branding You* and *StorySelling*. For free copies of their bestselling books and a special Celebrity Expert Resource featuring Nick, J.W., Brian Tracy, Tom Hopkins, and Michael Gerber, visit www.CelebrityBrandingAgency.com.

CHAPTER 15

A Demonstration of Brand vs. Brand + Direct Response

by Dan S. Kennedy

I read between 30 and 60 different industries' trade journals every month—some because I have clients in those fields, others just because they interest me or often contain information and ideas that might be useful to GKIC Members or because, as a stock market investor, I might gain investing insight. I read *Nation's Restaurant News* even though I don't own a restaurant. I read the Farm Bureau newspaper even though I'm not a farmer. I read *Variety*, the weekly trade journal of the entertainment industry, even though I'm not an actor, singer, or movie producer, although I am a long-term stockholder in Disney and at the time of this writing in the movie company Lionsgate.

FIGURE 15.1

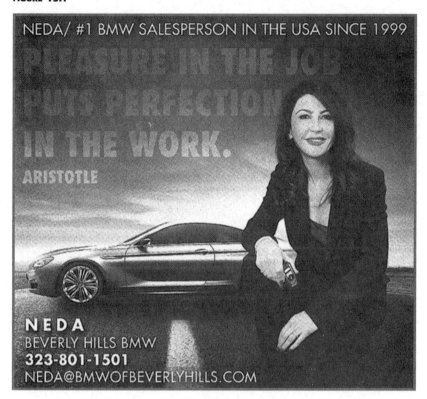

Anyway, the ad shown in Figure 15.1 (above) runs frequently in *Variety*. It is an ad for a car saleswoman. I do not know her and I have no idea how well the ad performs, or if she knows, and since it is a branding ad and not a direct-response ad, it's likely she doesn't. I plucked the ad to critique here, as I sometimes do ads for my five newsletters. It has no copyright, and heck, maybe you'll like it, you live in Hollywood, and you'll buy a car. She looks like a nice lady, and I can help her here, free of charge.

Variety is read by lots of affluent, image-conscious actors, producers, and agents who need to make a good impression with everything they do, including the car they drive.

Advertising here could be very good Place Strategy, and she is the only advertiser in her category, so she's practicing my favorite Place Strategy: Show Up Alone. Kudos for all that. She's reaching the kind of customers who want to deal with super-successful people, so her noting at the top of the ad that she is the number-one BMW salesperson since 1999 is a smart proclamation. Visually, the ad is eye-catching and artful. You won't be able to see it as well in this copy on uncoated book paper, as the original is on the slick magazine paper, but there the blue sky looks real, the words "Pleasure In The Job Puts Perfection In The Work" from Aristotle are transparent, so the sky is seen behind them yet they are perfectly legible. The car is sleek and shiny. Neda looks good. She's dressed in a navy blue or black business suit that fits her perfectly, there's just a hint of sexiness, nice smile. The ID in the lower left corner is in white against the steel blue-grey of the road surface. The whole thing looks terrific. It speaks of class and luxury.

This is the kind of personal brand ads you see a lot of real estate agents, financial advisors, cosmetic surgeons, and other professionals often pour money into—which I strongly discourage. They are fine as far as they go, and this one is an excellent example of such a brand ad. But they do not specifically invite you to do anything. This is like meeting her at a cocktail party, being introduced, having her tell you she is the number-one BMW salesperson, then abruptly spinning on her heel and walking away or, if you ask her a question, standing there mute. Or, a better analogy, since we are in sales, is having her knock on your door, introduce herself as the number-one BMW salesperson, spin, and walk away.

The other problem is that this lovely lady is paying this ad to show up in *Variety* for her, but not requiring it to prove it is earning its cost. To her credit, she hasn't loaded it up with Facebook, LinkedIn, and Twitter doorways to make accountability impossible. She's offered only two ways to respond, both direct, and she can obviously ask prospects where they heard of her. Still, there's a lot of room for leakage. And if she's running the same ad in multiple places, it gets murkier.

But the big, big, big flaw is that this ad only gets immediate response from buy-now customers. It does nothing and offers nothing for the many more who she has intrigued, who are just beginning to think about a new car, who plan to start shopping for a new car when their next residual check comes in. They are left loose, in the hope that imbedding her brand in their minds will be enough 4, 8, 10, 20 weeks later when they are ready to get new wheels. She has paid for those eyeballs to look at this ad, but she has no idea how many or who they are, and can do nothing to build trust and interest with them between now and the time they will actually buy a car.

Don't waste eyeballs you pay for.

Three Ways to Fix this Ad

The least aggressive option does absolutely zero damage to the branding or to the luxury image this ad conveys. We are not going to plunk a big red-and-white cardboard bucket of chicken down on the silver platter on the pure silk tablecloth in the mansion dining room. I'm not going to replace her elegant suit with a red, yellow, and white circus clown outfit and stick a red bulb nose on her. She does not need to commit image suicide. The ad can be shrunk vertically just a tiny bit, just enough to fit a line or two of direct-response copy, black or even grey on white at its bottom. It can be in a discreet and elegant typeface like this:

> To see a BMW test drive with Neda and a fascinating movie stunt man, visit DrivingWithNeda.com. For a Free Report, *How*

To Own The Perfect Luxury Automobile, and a DVD including a visit to the BMW factory to see the artisanship and have its incomparable technology demonstrated, complete the quick request form at www.DrivingWithNeda.com.

By adding these two offers, we create what's called Secondary Reason For Response. We give the person not ready right now to buy a car a reason to respond now anyway. To understand what to do with them when they arrive and how to place them in a good sales funnel, consult Chapter 30 of my *No B.S. Marketing to the Affluent* book, including the funnel diagram. Here, these points: One, Neda still gets the buy-now customers who call her or email her, but she also gets names, at least email addresses, and for the second offer, full addresses of not-ready-now potential buyers that she can continue communicating with directly.

Again, I haven't harmed the beauty of her main presentation in the slightest. Her personal brand is unscathed.

A more aggressive option would be to add a promise/benefit headline to the top or/and place a small testimonial from a famous Hollywood figure in the dead lower right corner AND add the same lead-generation offers I added above.

The most aggressive option would be to replace the entire ad with a black on white, article-look mini advertorial, matching the content typeface of the magazine, actually saying something. That headline might be "The #1 BMW Salesperson In The USA Since 1999 Announces Openings For Seven Hollywood/Beverly Hills Area Clients In Her Exclusive Private Client Group." The article would end with a direct call to action, to call or email her for Private Client details, a test drive, and a gift of fine wine with the test drive, and it would still have the Secondary Reason For Response Offers as well.

I doubt I'd ever convince Neda to buy this third option. I'd be seen as an uncouth beast. But maybe I can persuade you?

How to Accelerate Brand-Building Speed and Buy More Brand-Building Power

Let's assume that one of the above three methods results in the sale of, on average, one more car per month than she presently sells via this ad. Let's assume that equates to a few thousand dollars of commission income. What might Neda do with the money? She could go shopping on Rodeo Drive, but I'll bet her closet's already full. So, she could use it to buy a bigger ad. And if that upped sales yet again, she could go all the way up to a full page, cut in half vertically or horizontally, with a big image ad like hers in half its space and a constantly changing advertorial like I suggested in the other half of the space. With this much bigger presence, she'd be impossible not to notice and remember, and her brand would dominate faster, with more people.

That's how direct-response can build a brand, bigger, stronger, faster.

He *or she* who spends the most, the most wisely, does win. But few can spend the most out-of-pocket. By ramping up the proceeds of direct response, someone can spend more and more and more in more places or more often and achieve ultimate brand domination with a market.

Another way to think about this is to envision the paid-for but wasted eyeballs in the eye sockets of not-ready-now prospects who get away and later buy a car from someone else as dead weight your advertising budget has to haul around on its back. The dead weight grows heavier every time the ad runs. Soon it brings the ad budget to its knees. Our ad budget moves slower and more laboriously, bent over and crippled. If we liberate it and lift off the dead weight and convert the dead weight to energy drinks the ad budget consumes as it goes along, it can grow bigger and stronger, stand taller, and move faster. You decide whether or not to load it down with dead weight or to liberate it and power it up with your decisions about brand/image-only versus brand/image-with-direct response or direct response with brand/image, Secondary Reason For Response, and a good follow-up sales funnel.

CHAPTER 16

Your Brand Is Your Story:

How to Build Your Brand and Your Business by StorySelling™

by Nick Nanton and J.W. Dicks,
Celebrity Branding Agency

The marketing director of one of the biggest fast-food chains in the world had a problem on his hands. His biggest competitive advantage was probably that his food was a whole lot healthier than his rivals'—but his research was pretty clear that promoting that advantage wasn't going to do a whole lot for the chain's sales.

He knew he could go out there with all sorts of statistics and health information and make the case—but, those numbers and facts would just bore consumers, who only considered stopping in at one of his eateries for a quick meal when they were short on either money or time, or possibly both.

That meant the marketing director wasn't particularly excited when a Chicago franchisee found out about some guy who dropped a lot of pounds by only eating their food and took the story to the chain's ad agency. Again, they weren't promoting themselves as the fast-food equivalent of Jenny Craig or anything like that, so what good would that do? Not only that, but this kind of campaign could get the company in legal hot water. Their lawyers were warning that they could be in for a ton of liability lawsuits should they make any kind of health claims or promises.

The ad agency was insistent that this was a great idea, however. They put together a legal disclaimer that the lawyers could live with. So the marketing director finally sighed and agreed to try a regional test campaign.

Jared Fogle, a guy who lost 245 pounds eating the exact same Subway sandwich every day for months, appeared in his first commercial on January 1st, 2000—and the next thing he knew Oprah was booking him on her show. The marketing director was astounded by the instant success of the campaign, and it was soon rolled out nationally.

During the next ten years, Subway's sales doubled, the chain moved up from being the number-four fast-food franchise (after McDonald's, Burger King, and Wendy's) to become number three (displacing Wendy's), and Jared became a minor celebrity.

Not only that, but every time Subway tried to dump Jared from advertising, their sales suffered. The first time, in 2005, sales immediately fell by 10%. Jared's story was now Subway's—and it made them billions of dollars in the process.

The success of the Jared campaign is surely based on the premise of our first book, *Celebrity Branding You: "People Buy People."* When you effectively promote a real, living, breathing human being that people can connect with, as opposed to dry facts, the audience is going to be a lot more responsive just because of that "human touch."

And when you combine that personality with a compelling story, you've hit a marketing home run.

That's just what Subway did with Jared, who's a perfect example of the potential StorySelling™ holds for a business. He crystallized for consumers what ordinary nutritional information could never have accomplished: He provided an authentic story that visually demonstrated the benefit of eating at Subway (as long as, of course, you took it easy on the mayo, bacon, and cheese!).

But why was Jared necessary to make that kind of impact? Why couldn't simple and verifiable health facts deliver the same message—and, in turn, motivate the same rise of sales?

For that answer, we have to examine the power of stories—and how that power could dramatically increase your branding and sales success.

Storytelling: It Never Goes Out of Style

Cave drawings were the first way we came up with to tell a story. Those later evolved into hieroglyphics in ancient Egypt. Of course, you can only tell so much with pictures—and it can be a real drag having to sketch everything out. That's why, around 3,000 B.F. the Sumerian tribes in southern Mesopotamia developed the first primitive *writing*, which they called "cuneiform." Suddenly stories could be written in more detail—and that eliminated the guesswork involved in trying to figure out what those scrawls on those walls were trying to say.

Of course, most people back then couldn't read or write, which is why most stories were spread by simple word-of-mouth. This created a "survival of the fittest" process where the best stories ended up having an abnormally long shelf life, even though they only existed in oral form.

For example, around 500 ᴇ꜀., a fellow named Aesop was walking around delivering a great many memorable "fables"—stories that always had a moral lesson (or, as we call it today, a "takeaway"). It wasn't until *300 years later*, after its author was long dead and buried, that *Aesop's Fables* were actually written down and distributed.

The fact, however, remained that these and other powerful stories *refused to die*. There was something meaningful about them that motivated people to not only spread these stories far and wide, but also to hand them down to their children, and their children's children.

That's how the Bible came to be, of course; hundreds of years of oral storytelling finally resulted in holy men putting these tales together in the Old and New Testaments. The Bible also became the centerpiece of the next phase of storytelling, when Johannes Gutenberg created what we know as the modern printing press. Of course, it's not so modern anymore due to computers.

Which brings us to the 20th century, where we saw the most rapid and transformational change in storytelling. What we now know as "Old Media" was brand-new then—movies, radio, and TV were suddenly able to tell us stories in new and exciting ways. And, of course, the 21st century has brought even more incredible storytelling tools, through the explosion of "New Media"—online video, social media, blogs, websites, and more.

Stories are more important to us than ever. An effective narrative, even if it's found in a simple YouTube video, can quickly go viral throughout the world—indicating the public is feverishly searching for great stories more than at any other time in history. Aesop, if he were around today, would no doubt have his own Tumblr blogsite that would attract millions (especially if his fables featured the Kardashian family instead of turtles and birds).

> **DAN KENNEDY'S COMMENT**: In my field, success education, there have been two enduring stories so powerful that they refuse to die, and are told and retold by so many so often that they have kept books first published in 1937 and 1960, respectively, thriving to this day. The stories are what are called Origin Stories, and they are attached to Napoleon Hill and the book *Think And Grow Rich* and Dr. Maxwell Maltz and *Psycho-Cybernetics*, which I updated in a co-authored edition, *The New Psycho-Cybernetics*. In the health field, the example Nick and Jack just presented of Jared probably trumps all others, although you would also have to include the Charles Atlas story of "the bully who kicked sand in the face of the 90-pound weakling." Both are Transformation Stories. The best-known business Origin Story may be Disney's. Every business or product category, interest category, or field has at least several of these stories that never die and hold their value and influence over years, decades, generations. These are the stories to study as you craft your own.

This Is Your Brain on Stories: Why We're Addicted

The question remains—*why* do we like stories so much? Actually, change that, because we don't just *like* stories—we *love* them.

Literally.

Researchers at the Center for Neuroeconomics Studies at Claremont Graduate University, in Claremont, California[1],

---

[1] Jorge A. Barraza and Paul J. Zak, "Empathy Toward Strangers Triggers Oxytocin Release and Subsequent Generosity," *Annals of the New York Academy of Sciences*, June 2009.

discovered that stories activate the oxytocin hormone in our brains—this is actually *called* "the love hormone" by the scientific community. That's because it's associated with romantic attachment, human bonding . . . and yes, sex.

In other words, stories are way sexy. Even when they themselves are very far from it. Dr. Paul Zak, one of the Claremont researchers, showed volunteers a video that told a story about a four-year-old boy with terminal brain cancer— and also showed the same group a video of the same length about a four-year-old boy going to the zoo without any real narrative to it. Those that watched the first video had a 47% higher level of the love hormone. "Of all the stimuli we've developed that release oxytocin, this one was the best," said Zak of the story experiment.

Why do stories trigger that kind of reaction? Other research suggests that it happens because we identify with whoever the story is about—and put ourselves in their shoes. After all, we're all people—and we all experience the same fears, desires, joys, and ambitions.

More fun with brain scanning confirms that this is true. Jeffrey Zacks of Washington University in St. Louis, Missouri, ran functional magnetic resonance imaging (fMRI) scans of people reading a story or watching a movie[2]—and discovered that, when the main character encountered a situation, it activated the same parts of the brain in the subjects that would have responded if they themselves had been in the same predicament in real life. And it didn't matter if the story was read or experienced through a movie or a video—it was the content of the story itself that provoked the reaction.

---

[2] Gerry Everding, "Readers Build Vivid Mental Simulations of Narrative Situations, Brain Scans Suggest," www.phys.org, January 26, 2009.

We are addicted to stories in a very real sense—and here's more research that proves it. Read Montague of Virginia Tech University in Blacksburg, Virginia, and William Casebeer of the U.S. Defense Advanced Research Projects Agency (DARPA) in Arlington, Virginia,[3] analyzed how listening to a story affects the brain's reward centers—the parts that respond to such wonderful things as sex, good food, and drugs. Casebeer's conclusion? "If I were a betting man or woman, I would say that certain types of stories might be addictive and, neurobiologically speaking, not that different from taking a tiny hit of cocaine," says Casebeer.

Simply put, strong stories key into our emotions in a deep and profound way; we identify with them in a way we don't identify with raw data. That's why Jared's miracle sandwich diet was so effective for Subway—and also why raw black-and-white information wouldn't have been. Consumers could *see* that eating at Subway actually caused a person like them to lose weight—and, most importantly, could see it working for *them*. They identified with Jared—and it made for a very rewarding experience for their reward centers.

Splitting the Difference

Beyond the emotional component, however, stories actually accomplish a critical *function* for our brains. Believe it or not, *we need them to figure out our lives.*

Let's switch up researchers to find out just why this is—and examine the work of neuroscientist Michael Gazzaniga from the University of California, Santa Barbara. Gazzaniga has done incredible research in the whole right brain-left brain arena. He's the person who discovered that the mind's right

---

[3] Jessica Marshall, "Gripping Yarns," *New Scientist*, February 12, 2011.

side was more artistic, creative, and visual, while the left side was more verbal and intellectual (and he did this at the ripe old age of 25).[4]

Now, given that the right side of the brain was the artistic and creative half, that half would be the one that would naturally respond best to stories in whatever form they take, right?

Wrong—and this is where it gets interesting.

You see, Gazzaniga also discovered that you could actually separate the left side of the brain from the right, and the left side wouldn't suffer any loss in IQ points. Don't ask us how he found that out. We're afraid it will sound like a horror movie we definitely do not want to watch. Ever.

But something about the brain's ability to seemingly function the same, even when split in half, confused the good doctor. It didn't add up—if the different sides of our brains acted that independently, what accounted for our unity of thought, action, and purpose?

To find out, Gazzaniga used his access to people who had had surgery to disconnect communication between the two halves of their brains (this is done sometimes for severe epileptics, for example). What he discovered was equally revolutionary.

Whatever information he gave to the right side of the brain, the *left* side of the brain would then work overtime to explain. The left side, through storytelling, concocted narratives to make sense of random information. More research confirmed his initial results: Gazzinga began to call the left side of our brains "The Interpreter"—because a big part of its job is to put together individual facts to make a complete mental "picture."

---

[4] Benedict Carey, "Decoding the Brain's Cacophony," *The New York Times*, October 31, 2011.

In other words, the artistic half of our brains doesn't come up with the stories—the intellectual half does. And not as a creative pursuit—*but just as a way to make sense of what was happening all around it.*

Think about your own daily life. Think about how many times you try to explain to yourself (or to someone who's with you) something random that happens.

For example . . . you hear a random piece of gossip about someone acting strangely. You immediately try to connect the dots to solve the riddle of why that person acted out of character, and come up with excuses like, "They're getting a divorce," "They're on drugs," or maybe, "They lost their job."

Or . . . your car makes a funny noise on the way home from the store. You immediately try to formulate an explanation in your head for why it's making that sound. Needs an oil change. Maybe the muffler's loose.

Or . . . you watch TV shows like *CSI, NCIS,* or *Bones*—hourlong shows that have a central mystery at their core in each episode. These shows are so popular (just as murder mysteries and detective novels have traditionally been) because the audience is constantly trying to figure out the solution to whatever bizarre crime is being dramatized.

This tendency gets even more intense with a show like *Mad Men* or *Homeland,* shows that have an ongoing storyline. Something shocking happens at the end of the episode—and you spend the week trying to concoct the storyline that led up to the cliffhanger (and not just you—there are 50 million people on the internet also blogging and commenting, also trying to explain what happened).

Now, the above examples have something very much in common. In all instances, you pretty much *have no idea what the real story is.* But, the sad truth is . . . *you can't stop your brain from trying to figure it out anyway.*

That's your left side talking. It wants to know. It NEEDS to know.

Early man, pre-science, would make up various "gods" to explain away all kinds of natural happenings. That's because, at that time, humans weren't capable of discovering that the earth was round and it rotated—and *that's* why the sun came up in the morning and sank down in the evening.

But they *still had to know why.*

So they made up stuff. They filled in the blanks, just like we do every day.

It may be hard for you to think of Subway's Jared as an ancient god, but, in a sense, he was. He personified Subway's healthy eating possibilities and provided a living explanation of how they might work through his very dramatic weight-loss story. He filled in the blanks in a way that had impact. So people bought his StorySelling™—and, more importantly to the company, they subsequently bought a lot of Subway sandwiches.

As we've hopefully demonstrated, a myriad of scientists and researchers (along with all of human history as well!) have all come up with the same conclusion about stories: that certain ones really *do* answer primal needs that we all need to have met.

That's what makes StorySelling™ so powerful. When done correctly, it hits the human brain with an incredible impact, most of which is felt on a subconscious level. It also activates the pleasure centers of the brain—which makes you want to hear more.

Jared's diet breakthrough saga accomplished all that and more. It made a treat into a health food ("You mean you can lose weight by eating 6-inch subs?") and it created the perception that Subway's food wasn't just good to eat, it was also good *for* you.

The campaign was as effective as it could have possibly been, simply because Jared's story was *true*—and yet unbelievable at the same time.

The Four Key Factors of StorySelling™

When you apply StorySelling™ techniques to your brand, you have the potential to maximize your impact on your audience—and you give yourself the greatest opportunity to persuade them of your value vs. your competition's.

There are four key factors that, when combined, create the perfect climate for StorySelling™ success:

1. Simplicity

How many stories do we hear in a day? How much information do we end up taking in? The answer to both of those questions is the same: a scary, crazy amount. That means if your story isn't simple and easy to grasp, most of us, unless we're already intensely interested in the story, aren't going to hang on to it. Our lives are too busy and our minds too cluttered to take in something that's not directly relevant to what we're dealing with at the moment. With Jared, the facts were clear and easy to process—the guy ate nothing but Subway sandwiches for months and lost a whole bunch of weight.

2. Authenticity

We are also bombarded with marketing campaigns night and day—and most of us can smell a sales pitch a mile off. If your story only seems like an effort to get your audience to buy—or, even worse, if it doesn't have the ring of truth—no one is going to take it seriously. Jared was obviously not a polished media pro when he started doing Subway commercials—and that worked in the campaign's favor. He seemed real because he *was* real—

and so was his story, as many in the media found out when they checked it out and verified in their reporting that it was true.

3. Visibility

Obviously, the public, or at the very least, your target audience, has to have access to the story you want to tell. There are a lot of channels you can utilize to deliver your narrative; the point is, you can't expect your potential leads to come to *you,* you have to find a viable way to bring your story to *them.* Subway obviously put a lot of money behind exposing Jared's story to the public and made sure everyone they could possibly reach heard about it.

4. Relevancy

It also has to be a story that people *want* to hear. As we noted with Jared's Subway commercials, viewers loved the idea that you could lose weight at a fast-food restaurant. Again, we have so many people out there trying to sell us *their* stories that we block out as many as we can, just to keep our sanity. That means your narrative must be one that your audience is predisposed to hear for one reason or another—and that reason should be a powerful one.

Just like with any other powerful force, StorySelling™ is awesome to use—as long as you can maintain some control over it. Often, that's not possible. Ten years into Jared's run as a Subway spokesperson, for example, he ended up packing on a few pounds—which wasn't good for the campaign, which kept trying to cover up the weight gain. There were even a few ads where Jared's waistline was disguised by big bulky coats.

When something like that happens, however, there are ways to continue your narrative and make it turn back in your favor. In Subway's case, they turned Jared's weight gain into a *positive*—as they had him train for the New York Marathon in a new ad campaign, which gave them an entirely new narrative to StorySell™ with their sandwich star (and also guaranteed that he would again be svelte and commercial-ready!).

So think about what story you're telling with your brand—and look closely at it to see if it's really the most effective one you can tell. If you're not putting the power of StorySelling™ behind your brand, you're missing out on your single strongest opportunity to deliver your message in the most memorable way—and with the most profitable results!

NICK NANTON and **J.W. DICKS** lead The Celebrity Branding Agency®. Nick is an Emmy-winning documentary film director and producer, a gifted and skilled business storyteller, and an exceptionally knowledgeable media insider. J.W. Dicks is a strategic business development advisor and a securities and franchise attorney. They have perfected systems for personal and business credits. They are also the authors of *Celebrity Branding You* and *StorySelling*. For free copies of their bestselling books and a special Celebrity Expert Resource featuring Nick, J.W., Brian Tracy, Tom Hopkins, and Michael Gerber, visit www.CelebrityBrandingAgency.com.

RESOURCES

Nick and J.W. have a brand-new book, *Hollywood Secrets Revealed—How to Sell witout Selling by Telling Your Brand Story* providing much greater depth and detail on this important subject, available at all booksellers. If you'd like to hear a FREE AUDIO PROGRAM with Dan Kennedy; famed mystery novelist Les Roberts, with whom Dan collaborated on the novel *Win, Place or Die*; Nick Nanton; Donna Krech; and Lee Milteer, visit www.nobsbooks.com. Dan Kennedy also has a complete home study course on Influential Writing, and information about it can be found at www.DanKennedy.com/store.

CHAPTER 17

The Mouse and the Bunny

by Dan S. Kennedy

Walt frequently reminded everybody that "It all started with a mouse"—which he first named Mortimer and changed to Mickey at his wife's urging. Hef's empire began with a stag as a symbol of maleness, abandoned because it was already taken, so replaced by the symbol of eternal horniness, the rabbit. You can make the case his success actually began with Marilyn Monroe, but his brand-builder quickly became the bunny.

These are the two great brand-builders I've studied most carefully and admire most: Walt Disney and the keepers of his legacy and Hugh Hefner.

You might not think the two should share the same sentence, but they have a lot more in common than most people would imagine. In fact, Disney and Hefner were developing their businesses and brands in an overlapping time frame, and I feel confident they paid attention to each other with interest, and borrowed from each other liberally.

They both began with virtually no money to work with and built valuable, powerful, iconic brands with little investment in actual brand-building and virtually no brand/image advertising. Both Disney and Hefner grew their brands on the back of direct marketing and sales activity, on free advertising via media partnerships and publicity, and leverage of the media.

Other shared strategies include:

- *Creating a world of their own.* Walt's line "The Happiest Place On Earth" might have been used by Hefner for the world of Playboy, symbolized by the Playboy Mansion, if Walt hadn't already snagged it. Instead, we have actor Robert Culp's toast for the Mansion: "Gentlemen, gentlemen, be of good cheer, for they are out there and we are in here." The existential importance of The Playboy Mansion was shown off in a *Playboy* magazine cartoon, circa 1960, in which a truth-seeker has climbed to a mountain peak to beg wisdom from the wise guru at the top of the mountain. The guru tells him: "There is a man who lives in a mansion full of beautiful women and wears pajamas all the time. Sit at *his* feet and learn from him, for he has found the secret of true happiness." Walt also featured a symbolic structure at Disneyland, and again at Disney World: Sleeping Beauty's Castle, where dreams come true and romance flourishes. Both Disney and Playboy feature a profound sense of place— where no one ever need grow up.

- *Standing for and promoting a philosophy.* Hefner even called it "The Playboy Philosophy," and explained it in detail, beginning with a series of wordy essays extending over many months' issues of the magazine. Hefner argued against censorship, for sexual freedom, for civil rights, even for modern feminism. He also created a series of internal ads titled "What Sort of a Man Reads Playboy?," which presented a profile worthy of aspiration. Yes, readers were attracted by the pictures and the sex, but they *did* read the articles, including serious ones. Walt Disney also stood for certain enunciated principles and values, built into the films and entertainment product, taught by Walt, and integrated into projects like Epcot and Celebration. Here are a few revealing Walt Disney quotes:

  > "Disneyland would be a small world in itself—it would encompass the essence of the things that are good and true in American life . . . a place for people to find happiness and new knowledge. The older generation can capture the nostalgia of days gone by, the younger generation can savor the challenge of the future, and it will be a source of hope and inspiration to all the world."

  Rather a grandiose way to describe an amusement park, don't you think? But that's the point. Walt Disney and Hugh Hefner both saw and spoke of significance and importance in what they were doing that went far beyond the basic products and deliverables of their businesses. One more from Walt: "Since the beginning of mankind, the fable-tellers have not only given us entertainment, but a window to wisdom, a way to understanding." Whether you agree with them or not, these men who built great brands believed they were doing something important.

- *Personality-driven brand.* Walt was as much the public face of the Disney enterprises as was his creation Mickey. He began promoting Disneyland by hosting a show on ABC, and remained a familiar TV host for many years. The public came to know, admire, and love Walt, and masses wept and mourned the day of his death. He was the company's chief storyteller and salesman. Hugh Hefner used his own TV show early, purportedly a party in his own penthouse living quarters, with his celebrity buddies all there having a good time. Very recently, after decades, he was seen again starring, with his girlfriends, at the Mansion, in a reality TV series. The two individuals and these two brands, inseparable.

- *Cast of characters.* Walt and Mickey, Minnie, Pluto, Goofy, as well as Snow White, Cinderella, Mary Poppins, and the more contemporary Nemo, Belle, and The Beast, etc. Hefner with the Playboy bunnies, the Playmates of the Months, Playmates of the Years, his girlfriends, his celebrity friends. When the Disney company acquired Marvel, its CEO, Bob Iger, said, "You can never have too many good characters." Hefner has felt the same way about girlfriends.

- *Place.* The Disney Parks with Cinderella's Castle as centerpoint. The Playboy Mansion, with its infamous Grotto as its centerpoint. Both sites have a "Fantasyland"!

- *Product as Promotion.* For Disney, it began with a licensed Mickey Mouse watch and a Disney train, both products credited with rescuing the companies involved from financial struggle. Disney, of course, has become a licensing juggernaut, with its characters and iconic images on hundreds of thousands of products. The Playboy bunny logo is one of the most licensed trademarks of any, of all time, for apparel, cologne, artwork, etc., and just like Mickey and Minnie, caricatures of Playboy bunnies have made their way to statues, dolls, posters, apparel, even custom motorcycles. All this proliferate product not only generates revenues, but it works at promoting and creating and sustaining interest in the brand.

- *Media.* Walt Disney literally launched Disneyland with what he first considered an unholy alliance with ABC— now Disney owns them, along with ESPN and several Disney-branded cable TV channels and Disney radio stations, but, also, still airs Disney parades and specials on ABC, each an infomercial for the parks, current Disney personalities, and new movies. Hugh Hefner began with his own media, *Playboy* magazine, but, as noted, promoted Playboy early with TV. To this day, he still uses such media plays—in recent years, there was one reality show, and briefly two, on the E Network, all about the Mansion and his girlfriends. There was a feature film, in 2008, *The House Bunny*. It was produced by Adam Sandler's company, Happy Madison, and included stars like Emma Stone, Anna Faris, and Colin Hanks. It debuted at number one at the U.S. box office its first week, number one in the U.K., but ultimately managed just $70 million gross against a $22 million production budget—and it was savaged by critics. Regardless of critics' opinions or level of success, all these serve as powerful infomercials for the brand, yet Playboy has been paid for them rather than buying advertising. Its own cable TV channel is also both a business itself and continuous, 365-day brand promotion.

I've Followed the Disney/Hefner Model and You Can, Too

Looping back, consider how these two men launched and built their brands. They never spent or had to spend on dopey image advertising. Their brands were built by their own media products and businesses, by profitable advertising selling their products, by stealth advertising imbedded in TV programming they were paid to produce and provide or paid licensing fees for, and by an untold variety of merchandise proliferating in the marketplace, for which they were also paid licensing fees.

In much the same way, I have built my brands. I have never once spent a nickel on a "Who Is Dan Kennedy?" or "What Is GKIC?" brand/image advertisement. I have been paid to build my business and my brand, in cash—as with book royalties, article fees, revenue from info-products, speaking fees, and on-site info-product sales at speaking appearances, etc., or in free advertising—as with products featured in others' catalogs, syndicated articles published in niche industry leaders' newsletters, being interviewed on countless business-thought leaders' audio programs and tele-seminars, and book tours paid for by corporate sponsors. Through these means, I reach more than one million business owners a year without a penny of out-of-pocket investment. I have also baked in every other strategy shared by Disney and Playboy described in this chapter.

Martha Stewart is another example of someone who built a powerful and valuable brand from which she has extracted many, many millions of dollars, using fundamentally this same approach, and Rachael Ray has closely followed her model. Incredibly, Martha Stewart's company has failed to turn a profit for the past six years, and there's a cautionary tale there for another place and time, but she has personally amassed considerable wealth. And her personal brand had such a strong and passionate following even a stint in federal prison failed to dent her popularity.

If you have a small, local business you may too quickly disqualify yourself and think that this is above and beyond you. There are two things to consider about that. One is that everybody started and starts somewhere, often small and local. Disneyland was, after all, a local business, and central Florida was picked as the second location based on the population within one day's driving distance. There was no thought initially of global domination. Hefner began in Chicago, his office in his apartment, his magazine assembled atop his bed, and then with one local Playboy Club. Also, these days, geographic boundaries have been blurred and expanded if not erased by ecommerce and overnight shipping. A local gourmet cupcake store in Hudson, Ohio, has customers in 40 states and 9 countries. A clothier's shop in London, England, Charles Tyrwhitt, mails catalogs throughout the U.S.—including to me, and ships shirts and ties worldwide. Why must *you* think small?

RECOMMENDED READING

The Disney Way by Capodagli and Jackson

Inside The Magic Kingdom by Connellan

The Vault of Walt: Unofficial, Unauthorized, Uncensored Disney Stories Never Told by Korkis

Disney U. by Lipp

How To Be Like Walt by Williams

The Quotable Walt Disney by Disney Editions

Think Outside The Box by Vance and Deacon

Hef's Little Black Book by Hugh Hefner with Bill Zehme

Second, even if choosing to be local, and stay small, all the same strategies can and should apply, particularly if you want to be a locally dominant brand. Why shouldn't *you* dominate your market?

Figure 17.1 below is the cover of an issue of my *Renegade Millionaire Magazine,* featuring a profile of Hugh Hefner. The current number-one Dan Kennedy publication is *The No B.S. Marketing Letter,* and you are invited to sample it free, via the offer on page 261.

FIGURE 17.1

CHAPTER 18

Building a Brand by Building Bonfires

by Dan S. Kennedy

Media publicity, social media buzz, what EST's Werner Erhard dubbed "sell it by zealot"—now viral buzz by brand loyalists, deliberately or accidentally ignited public conversation can be as dangerous as playing with dynamite and lit matches in a moving pickup truck on a bumpy dirt road, but it can also be a way to accelerate brand-building and to activate more brand loyalists as evangelical recruiters.

The old joke about there being no such thing as bad publicity is no longer universally true. For celebrities, it's a very unpredictable thing. Celebrity cook Paula Deen's publicized use of the "N word" seems, as of this writing, to have severely damaged her brand and business and set endorsers fleeing, but it did also, immediately, spark a huge surge of purchases of her cookbooks at Amazon. Tiger Woods similarly saw his sponsors withdraw en masse, but it appears, at this point, that he may yet be resurrected as a commercial spokesperson. I'll court danger by saying so, but overall, painting with broad brush, it's my observation that the media is more eagerly forgiving of black celebrities' controversial statements and bad behavior than they are of white celebrities who get into similar difficulty. For companies, controversy and/or bad news and bad press can be even more dangerous, yet many brands are surprisingly resilient, and many even benefit from dynamite exploding in their hands.

One thing that the internet has created, that's important to understand, is a remaking of publicity, media exposure, public discussion, and gossip as direct-response marketing, because it's easy for interested people to find you. It's very easy, for example, to find me, if anything seen or read or heard anywhere piques your curiosity. You just type my name into Google. Or Amazon. Or Facebook. Before the internet, this was not the case. Guests on talk shows, for example, had to fight to get an 800 number given out, and were often denied that opportunity. If you were interviewed and included in a magazine article, there was no easy way for readers to locate you or contact you. They might go to a store and ask about your product, but if it wasn't there, that ended that. They might go to a bookstore, but if you weren't the author of a book currently in print, that ended that. Today, you are essentially walking, talking direct-response media. Even a brief mention of your brand in the media can send people on an immediately fruitful search of you. If, for example, there was no contact information of any kind provided in this book for Nick Nanton, but a few sentences I wrote about him interested you, how hard would it be for you to find him and his company online? It takes me longer to microwave my morning cup of coffee.

With this in mind, it's vital to understand direct-response and direct-marketing funnels, so that when people do find you on their own, by whatever provocation, or none but organic search, the trail leads them to and through a door, onto a pathway with high walls on either side, to a series of yes/no actions, ultimately converting them to viable prospects and the highest percentage of them possible to customers. Traffic and visitor counts are, frankly, B.S., flung about by fools and social media promoters and charlatans like monkeys at the zoo fling feces. It's meaningless. Only traffic converted to prospects and customers, converted to sales and profits count. Be very wary of all the "new metrics" gobbledygook. There's no line for it on a bank deposit slip. If the construction of marketing funnels for lead capture and conversion is foreign to you, it will very quickly be made clear when you accept my free offer on page 261.

Also, with this in mind, it's important to understand that there are no longer any protective walls around your brand. It is exposed 24/7/365. And the impact of whatever is said or happens is instant and may spread at the speed of light. There is no news cycle anymore. There's just news now. You can manipulate and use the talk about you more aggressively than ever before. You can also be damaged by it more harshly and more quickly than ever before.

Brand protection includes internal law enforcement. My book, *No B.S. Guide to Ruthless Management of People and Profits*, is the bluntest, toughest instruction manual for brand protection from the inside out ever written by anybody. In it, for example, I recommend full audio and video surveillance of every person who interacts with customers in every place they interact with customers, frequent "mystery shopping" of the answering of your phones, carefully constructed scripts and enforcement of their use, rapid-fire response to mistakes and consumer dissatisfaction, firing fast and hiring slow, and other important measures to protect profit margins and to protect brand. This is the part of business ownership and management people like the least, fear the most, and do the worst. From a brand-equity standpoint, any problem or problem employee not nipped in the bud can bring the entire enterprise to disaster.

The more successful and visible you are, the more important this is. If you focus on brand-building but neglect brand protection, you will likely see, at some point, all your good efforts and investment turn to ruin.

With these cautionary notes made, let's take a look at how we might build your brand with new followers or with loyalists, by taking risks and playing with fire. After all, doesn't fortune favor the bold?

Your Brand and Controversy: Dare You Brand-Build by Being for or Against a Mainstream Issue?

In July 2012, the president of the Chick-fil-A fast-food chain told a Christian publication, *The Biblical Reporter*, that the company and its brand "supports the biblical definition of the family unit." A direct answer to a direct question by a writer for a relatively obscure news outlet made its way into the mainstream, and a major uproar ensued. The mayor of Chicago suggested that the company would not be welcomed if opening restaurants in the city. Liberal TV media like MSNBC attacked the company as bigoted and questioned whether or not its leaders' religious beliefs were creating a hostile workplace or workplace discrimination. A boycott was promoted. But on the flip side, Chick-fil-A brand loyalists and evangelical Christian groups rushed to the company's defense, organized "support days" at the restaurants, and overall, the company saw a year-to-year revenue increase from $4 billion to $4.6 billion. It isn't easy to get that kind of sales boost through regular advertising and growth. Much of it came directly from the heightened visibility and public conversation about the chain, and from the invigorated support of its customer base. If there is any lasting brand damage, it's invisible to me.

For the record, their position was no surprise. This is a company very well-known for closing its stores, even its stores inside malls, on Sunday to celebrate the Sabbath, and for beginning all its business meetings with prayer. Thinking they might be in favor of or even neutral about gay marriage is like thinking the Clint Eastwood movie character "Dirty Harry" might be worried over the difficult childhood of a criminal he cornered in an alley. Still, this rather trivial remark became a Major News Media Event, extended over several weeks, and organized warring groups lined up across from each other in Chick-fil-A parking lots and, more so, all over social media. When all the feathers settled, the net result was a substantial sales increase and a cementing of bond between the brand and its base.

On the other side of this same controversial issue, Howard Schultz, the CEO of Starbucks, received applause at the annual shareholders meeting in 2013 when he stated his and the company's unwavering support for same-sex marriage, reinforcing the company's already announced advocacy for same-sex marriage legislation dating to January 2012. That created a much smaller media firestorm and far less mainstream media criticism than did Chick-fil-A's opposing stand, but it did spark an organized "Dump Starbucks" boycott promoted by the National Organization for Marriage.

Regardless, Starbucks experienced nearly a 15% revenue growth in 2012, and continued success in 2013.

These two tales probably indicate that the core customer base owned by Starbucks is a significantly different core customer base than that owned by Chick-fil-A, and both have large armies of brand loyalists likely to agree with the stand taken by the company they already support. Knowing who your customers and who your brand loyalists are, how they line up on issues, who their heroes are, and who their enemies are is important. I'm not suggesting that the CEO, of Chick-Fil-A or of Starbucks aren't authentic and sincere in their conflicting viewpoints. I'm not accusing them of simple pandering. Mostly, I personally respect and admire both of them and their companies, and I like one's coffee and the other one's chicken. But they may both have been emboldened by a good understanding of their respective core constituencies. Courage in context is easier than courage in a vacuum.

The bigger and broader point is that a short-term media or social media reaction, pro or con or both, to a company or its owner, CEO, celebrity endorser, or other "face" taking a controversial position or otherwise getting into troubled waters often has little or no lasting negative impact and can, instead, have positive impact, in making a larger population aware of the brand or at least rallying the loyalists. Some entrepreneurs who own valuable personal or corporate brands even intentionally, repeatedly court controversy, like Kenneth Cole and American Apparel. Donald Trump finds somebody to pick a very public fight with anytime he wants media attention and publicity—his targets have included comedian Rosie O'Donnell and President Obama. Hugh Hefner fueled Playboy's rise with controversy. By its nature, the brand was controversial—although it seems quaint now, compared to everything else on the media landscape. But Hef ginned up controversy; he didn't try to tamp it down. In the description of Toby Keith's brand-building (see Chapter 20), a similar strategy is revealed: risking and not worrying about controversy and criticism from media or noncustomers in order to strengthen brand loyalty with the base.

Of course, anytime you personally take a potentially controversial position or attach your company or brand to one, you *do* take risks. Not long ago, you could do it in communications only with your customers, members, or subscribers, or even in targeted media as Chick-Fil-A's president did, and never have it see the light of day with the public or the mainstream media. There is still some "spread" between what is said publicly and what is said to supporters and donors by politicians. If you get direct mail for candidates or from the RNC or DNC, you will sometimes see much more pointed and strident position taking and demonizing done there than by the same candidate or organization's spokespersons on the Sunday talk shows. But it is harder and harder to protect that firewall. Governor Romney got caught making derogatory remarks to donors in a closed-door meeting about the 47% of Americans on the dole, taped via a cell phone, and the incident did damage. In the prior campaign, Senator Obama had his disdainful remarks intended only for Left Coast donors about the voters in rural areas clinging to their guns and Bibles captured and made public, but he survived the damage. Cell phone cameras and video cameras, recording devices the size of a shirt button, social media welcoming unfiltered content and spreading it virally and rapidly, and mainstream media increasingly drawing its content from that social media produces an environment where nothing can be "off the record." If you are going to court controversy, you should do it consciously and deliberately, not casually or impulsively.

If You Punch Their Enemy in the Nose, You Are Their Friend

The Trump Technique of picking a fight with a villain or enemy can be an effective way to use controversy with little or no risk if you choose carefully, attack broadly, and know your brand loyalists and target market well. I, for example, have long done well with my audiences of "from scratch" millionaire, multi-millionaire, and up-and-coming entrepreneurs and sales professionals by attacking, vilifying, and mocking 1) pin-headed academics, academic theorists, and Ph.D.s (which stands for: Piled Higher and Deeper); 2) Big, Dumb Companies and their corporate suits; 3) Madison Avenue ad agencies; 4) slothful employees; 5) socialist-leaning critics of ambition, initiative, achievement, success and wealth; and 6) nanny-state meddlers. I can and have attacked Michael Moore, Mayor Bloomberg, Obamacare, named companies doing incredibly dumb advertising, etc., with abandon in my books, newsletters, and speeches, and been cheered. Good places to see this are in my books *No B.S. Ruthless Management of People and Profits*—starting right out in Chapter 1, and *No B.S. Sales Success in The New Economy* –notably in the chapter about sales managers. A lot of people are not consciously completely aware of how much of this I do, and how much I leverage it, but it is actually a major force fueling my own brand.

Life Extension, a major marketer of its own brand of nutritional supplements, uses its own magazine to frequently attack the FDA and the medical establishment. The magazine does have limited newsstand distribution, but it is primarily subscribed to, sent to, and written for its own customers, so its take on medical establishment, big pharma, and government conspiracy to suppress natural health cures is "preaching to the converted," a smart means of reinforcing and strengthening brand loyalty. Life Extension is certainly not alone in this approach in their industry, and when I write direct-response copy for clients in this field, I almost always incorporate the same enemies. They do it as well and aggressively as anybody, though, and can be seen at www. lifeextension.com.

Making Your Brand about a Movement, Not (Just) a Business

I have also worked hard to position myself as a leader of a movement—actually of movements—not just an entrepreneur out to make a buck. I have, in fact, led a movement toward direct-response advertising and direct marketing in hundreds of diverse industries and professions, including those where it was rarely seen or used before I lit the light and ignited the revolution. In more than a hundred fields, there are Dan Kennedy-created, taught, or directly influenced marketing "gurus," each directly guiding the marketing of thousands to tens of thousands of their industry's members to use of my kind of marketing. These include people like Ben Glass at Great Legal Marketing, Richard James at YourBusinessAutomated.com, and Ken Hardison at Personal Injury Lawyers Marketing Association (PILMA), each working with thousands of law firms; Craig Proctor and Kinder & Reese, each working with thousands of Realtors; Jay Geier at The Scheduling Institute, Dr. Tom Orent, and Greg Stanley at Whitehall Management, each working with thousands of dentists; and so on. Combined, we have created a tidal wave of change in these fields. This same change led by Kennedy-linked thought leaders, trainers, and marketing companies has permeated the auto retailing, auto repair, carpet cleaning, landscaping, home remodeling, restaurant, travel, insurance, financial services, chiropractic, cosmetic surgery, retail in just about every category, assisted living and nursing homes, even funeral parlors, as well as B2B environments, like software companies, industrial chemicals and supplies, and industrial equipment. Most of the business owners, company CEOs, private practice professionals, and sales professionals engaged in these groups downstream from me are familiar with my brands and understand they are part of a change movement in marketing, and they're proud of it. It's like being part of any revolution: It's self-validating, it's cool, it's exciting, it's daring. You can certainly see that the Iron Tribe guys have adopted very comparable positioning for their radical change movement in fitness and health.

I have always taken a position as a champion of "the little guy:" the small-business owner, the shopkeeper, the local service provider, the employer of 5 to 50, the true backbone and lifeblood of the economy. Also, the champion of the often-looked-down-upon salesman, who gets knocked down only to get up and knock on the next door, and in doing so, creates all the revenue that ultimately builds every university and hospital and backs every worker's paycheck. I tell them that any other group can take all the vacations they want and we'll still all get along, but if all the small-business owners or all the salespeople went to sleep for 30 consecutive days, the entire nation would grind to a halt. There'd be suffering, starvation, and, soon, rioting in the streets. These people are heroes. They eschew job security, comfort, 9-to-5ing in favor of investment and risk, constant uncertainty, long hours. They don't take jobs—they *make* jobs. They are part of the great entrepreneur movement, the independence and self-reliance movement. Here in the United States, they share legacy with the founders and builders of this nation.

When they are demonized as workaholics or evil, greedy capitalists or wild-eyed dreamers or some other stereotype, it is sometimes by the merely ignorant, but often by those of a competing movement toward a dependent, forcibly equalized, socialist state. Together, I and they carry not only the economy but the philosophy that made us a great society squarely on our shoulders. A business made prosperous is a burnishing of the Liberty Bell and a force for real social good, and earned wealth and privilege is admirable and deserved—for all success (and failure) is ultimately behavioral choice. With this sort of message, basically my brand message, I lift the self-esteem and sense of worth of my customers. We are in it together!

All this makes my personal brand and the business brands attached to me more *significant*. To brand loyalists, this is a source of pride, that they are associated and involved with something important, not just a customer of a business.

If you leap to the idea that it's easy for me to do this in my field, but, well, your business is different—it's ordinary, mundane, selling commodities, and you can't follow this path, I suggest looking at the clothing company Bills Khakis. You will see their "mission page" from their Summer 2013 catalog in Figure 18.1 on page 202. I'm sure they won't mind the publicity. Their brand is "cut and sewn in the USA," necessarily clever wording because some of the fabric itself may be imported. They began as a direct-response marketer, essentially a mail-order company, and used radio advertising on the ultra-conservative talker Glenn Beck's programs, in which they emphasized their status as "an authentic American sportswear company," to drive response. Today, they are a strong mail-order catalog company, an ecommerce company (www.BillsKhakis.com), and also have their products sold in

FIGURE 18.1: Bills Khakis Ad

SUMMER 2013

Bills Khakis was founded on one simple premise – it's almost impossible to find a great pair of khakis twice. Consistent with this same thought, it's almost impossible to find sportswear from a company that you can truly believe in - a brand that's an extension of you rather than the other way around. In our quality, enduring style, and commitment to American-made craftsmanship, it's our hope that you will wear Bills Khakis with a quiet, confident sense of pride. You wouldn't tell everyone you know about Bills Khakis but you might tell your best friend... simply because they deserve to know. Thank you for buying into our dream of building an authentic American sportswear company. Bills Khakis are also available through the finest independent men's specialty stores in the United States. You will find a listing of retailers who carry a wide selection of our products on the back inside cover of this catalog.

WE MADE BILLS BETTER BY NOT CHANGING A THING.®

Bill Thomas

Bill Thomas, Founder

Est. 1990

BILLSKHAKIS.COM   1-888-9-KHAKIS (1-888-954-2547)

hundreds of stores nationwide. They have latched onto the "Made In America Movement," in resurgence after a long sleep begun in the 1960s.

Similar movements that businesses can attach themselves to, which have current and rising influence, are "Support Local Businesses," "Homegrown Produce," and "Farm to Table," and nonprofit causes and the reputable charitable organizations associated with them, like support for veterans and the Wounded Warriors organization, or eradicating child hunger and the nation's or your local Food Bank. Steve Adams, who you've met in this book, does a fine job of linking his pet stores to animal rescue organizations, thus the movement against animal abuse.

Finding a Rising Tide

There are big, societal rising tides. Some come and go. Others are perennial. Patriotism is a rising tide. In a local community, its high school football team may be a rising tide, as the focus of the entire town's attention every Friday night for several months. Entrepreneurship has always been my rising tide. Obsession with celebrity is a rising tide, and the GKIC Members in the catering business included in Chapter 11 have risen with it with their local business, just as my long-time client Guthy-Renker Corporation rose with it from their very first TV infomercial as a startup to their multibrand, multidistribution-channel $1.8 billion business now. Home shopping TV was the rising tide for my one-time client Joan Rivers. Reality TV has recently been the rising tide for a number of otherwise rather obscure businesspeople, like the folks seen in *Pawn Stars* or *Duck Dynasty*. Hefner's rising tide was the sexual revolution of the 1960s. Limbaugh's rising tide was the Bill Clinton administration and his role as the number-one Voice of Opposition. In this chapter, we've discussed other rising tides.

Find yours.

CHAPTER 19

The Power of Paranoia and Death by a Thousand Cuts

by Dan S. Kennedy

My two favorite quotes about paranoia are "Only the paranoid survive," from Harold Geneen, once head of the once mighty ITT, and "Just because you're paranoid doesn't mean they're not out to get you," which I first heard from Dr. Charles Jarvis.

It's no fun walking around worried and paranoid, seeing evildoers lurking in the bushes everywhere you turn. We all prefer comfortable complacency. Most do not prepare for the walk across the shopping center parking lot having their Mace® or other weapon at the ready, taking care to walk closer to the middle than the rows of parked cars to avoid being easily yanked between autos by a waiting attacker. Most do not have a fire extinguisher on every floor of their homes, smoke detectors and heat detectors, preplanned escape routes. A small percentage of homes have "safe rooms." Most do not ask for hotel rooms on lower floors. Now, the younger people who've grown up living their lives online have little concern over privacy and think nothing of publicly displaying their lives, their children, their homes in social media and storing all their financial and personal information in some distant "cloud," despite hackers' theft of data being in the news on a near-daily basis.

A friend once told me, "You never really learn to always pull into your garage and wait until the door closes behind you before getting out of your locked car until you find yourself standing there facing three thugs who were waiting in the bushes, have a bag put over your head and your hands tied behind your back, and are shoved into your house to lie on the floor while they rob the place, rape your wife, and threaten your children."

A famous sales video in the fire alarm business was titled "Another Man's Family" because everybody thinks of things like fires and home invasion robberies and tall trees toppling over on them and teenage sons peddling drugs, etc., as happening only to other people's families.

The same embrace of comfortable complacency occurs in business, especially with companies with famous and powerful brands. All sorts of dangerous emotional states occur, from the boardroom in the office tower penthouse down to the store manager and secretary: the sense of inevitability. A sense of entitlement. Disdain for upstart competitors and odd, new ideas. Taking customers and customers' loyalty for granted. Resenting the need to work or sell or innovate.

Most people who think of Facebook as a permanent part of our lives have little or no memory of MySpace. Most people who think of Walmart in the same way have no memory of Woolworth's. Diners Club and Carte Blanche were once elite and successful credit card brands. I still have a Diners Club card, but it is really just a Mastercard. Carte Blanche, gone. Everybody knows McDonald's but Bob's Big Boy is a fading memory. Holiday Inns and Howard Johnson's once dominated the freeway-exit motel industry. It was briefly believed that People's Express was the airline destined to take over the industry. Kinney Shoes. Montgomery Wards. The graveyard of dead national brands and the once giant, even dominant companies they fronted is unimaginably large. There are more dead than alive in just about every category of commerce and industry.

No One Is Ever Really Safe

Brand is absolutely no assurance of success or longevity, nor insurance against sloth or stupidity. Brand as protective armor for the business battlefield is illusion. Legacy brands certainly exist and some thrive. Dating way back but still alive and valuable today, in my field, Dale Carnegie comes to mind. In the very busy diet industry where fads come and go and few survive as brands, Weight Watchers, once a client of mine, comes to mind. Tupperware. Disney, discussed in Chapter 17. The Rolling Stones are still on tour. But these are more notable exceptions than rule. If you create or come into possession of a valuable brand, you must then sleep with one eye open forevermore. A growing number of barbarians gather at your gates, surround your fortress walls. Barbarians because they lack respect for their elders, they are rude and brash and coarse and bold, they do not fear, and they will kill you and eat you and leave only bones behind without a twinge of remorse. Most brand owners who are destroyed first sow the seeds of their own destruction and create their own vulnerability. In many cases, they deserve to die.

Brands lose their luster and power many different ways.

- *Poor, worsening product quality and/or customer service and often a level of "don't bother me" arrogance about it does in a lot of big brands.* I would hang that on Holiday Inns and Howard Johnson's. It's what opened the door for the Japanese invasion of the auto industry in America. If you are under age 50, it's probably hard to imagine that people hated, reviled, and shunned the person in their neighborhood who dared to buy a Japanese car. These cars got keyed and vandalized in parking lots. And Japanese cars were widely viewed as pure crap. Now it seems no company can make cars. Rarely does a week go by without some company—from Ford to Hyundai—announcing a recall of 50,000 to 500,000 of their cars suffering some sort of defect. I owned one Ford Explorer that had four different recalls over five years. Cadillac and Lincoln once owned the aspirational buyer. They were the symbols of upward mobility and success in America. Producing defective and dysfunctional products, delivering poor service, serving up gruel and telling customers to eat it and like it creates great vulnerability. And no brand can long protect itself from such bad behavior.
- *Failure to be interesting puts brands at risk.* Way back in the 1950s, the folks running Proctor & Gamble realized that no matter how perfectly their flagship laundry detergent, Tide, performed, housewives simply got bored with it and bought other brands. Some returned periodically to Tide. Some were lost forever. They created a strategy, still used today, of making some minor "new and improved" tweak to Tide every 60 to 120

days—adding a scent, taking out all scent, adding fabric softener, changing the bottle, changing the cap, and so on. Some of the innovations have come, gone, returned, gone, and returned again many times. They have also created a number of different versions of Tide, so a consumer can move about within the brand's product line. They also created Tide in different bottles with different names to compete with themselves and still get the bored and wayward consumer's money. Surf, as example. An unimaginative substitute name for Tide, but one that sold well nonetheless. The fast-food chains each have their basic, fundamental menus, but just about all of them have borrowed Disney's strategy of limited release, then back in the vault, and periodically re-release a food item for a brief time then take it away—McDonalds' McRib Sandwich is a good example. Taco Bell has had a huge hit co-branding with Doritos, producing taco shells made from Doritos chips, and featuring them for a limited time.

One of the three most important marketing questions in business* is: *What's new?* There is damn little curiosity about what's the same as the last time the consumer visited,

---

RESOURCE

* There are two other equally important questions: *What's next?*—which has to do with either sequential progression or ascension. And, my copyrighted, proprietary Unique Selling Proposition question: *Why should I choose to do business with you versus any and every other option available to me?* If you would like a Free Special Report on "Ten Smart Marketing Questions to Discuss with Yourself," visit www.NoBSBooks.com and search for the resources tied to this book.

---

heard about, or read about a business. Un-curious, bored customers cannot long be held by a leash braided from brand.

A brand business can do a lot to keep itself interesting without real, groundbreaking innovation. Innovation carries risk, because it can take you away from what customers like best or trust most, but even with those risks, it's hard to avoid it entirely over a long term and still thrive. A lack of legitimate innovation leaves the best of brands vulnerable. All the pizza brands left themselves vulnerable to upstart Dominos because none of the established companies bothered with any solutions to the slow and unreliable delivery of cold pizza. Kodak, one of the most iconic of American brands, became virtually worthless by ignoring the digital revolution in photography. I am personally not much of an innovation guy, and I'm definitely, determinedly not a technology guy, but I have made a point of surrounding myself with, partnering with, and utilizing people and companies that are. One of the three chief motivators in play when I sold the publishing and information marketing business I'd built to Bill Glazer was the recognition that a great many things related to online media for marketing and product deliverables were fast becoming essential, and I wasn't willing to do them or helm them. This allowed me to continue focusing on—and even innovating in—aspects of this business I enjoy and that utilize my highest and best skills, but prevented the business as a whole from becoming stodgy and stale.

A brand can even become too well known. To a degree, Weight Watchers has long suffered from this. People widely credit it as the only diet program that actually works, but they also feel they know what it is about, how it works, and, unfortunately, that it is difficult. I've twice rescued a client from this fate in a niche market. Each time he had achieved for himself and his company what many would envy: four out of five in his market of some 90,000 people, if asked, would say only complimentary things, but could then list the five things he taught and was all about. So, no mystery, no curiosity, no interest. All kinds of credibility, but more a burden than a benefit. For this reason, twice, with my assistance, he has had to totally reinvent himself and his message, yet hold onto the credible and influential status of his well-built brand. He has had to become the extremely experienced, most trustworthy elder authority who has found and brought forward a legitimate, new, radical breakthrough in the field. It isn't an easy trick, marrying such a brand to new mystique. But it can be done.

My friend and colleague Sally Hogshead, wise in brand-making, but also smart about direct response, is the "guru" of fascination. In fact, she's the first and only person to develop research-based *science* for making yourself, your company, and your brand fascinating. I recommend her first book: *Fascinate: Your 7 Triggers to Persuasion and Captivation*. There is also a Fascinating Marketing System with modules she and I collaborated on, which you can get information about at: www.HowToFascinate.com.

Many people erroneously think of brand-building as a journey or sprint to a finish line of brand-achievement. The very idea that arrival counts for little and they must still and forever get out of bed every morning paranoid and hard at work at newly fascinating those now familiar with them seems obscenely unjust. As unhappy as these people are when they confront this nasty reality, they are even more unhappy when all they believe they've built so solidly dissolves like a sand castle at the first high tide. Fascination is not an accomplishment; it's a mandate.

Death by 1,000 Paper Cuts

Most big, famous, credible, popular brands do *not* die overnight, from a sudden burst of gunfire or bomb blast or single, epic error. In fact, good brands can have surprising resiliency. When a Carnival Cruise Lines ship in Italy crashed, tipped over, and ultimately sank, endangering and stranding passengers, I raced to buy some stock in the company. Despite a subsequent, even more news media spotlit disaster at sea, with an entire ship of passengers stranded for days on a powerless boat, with depleting food supplies, nonworking bathrooms, and uninhabitable conditions, that stock I bought has gone up in value and the company remains well afloat. Tylenol survived a poisoned product disaster. Taco Bell survived a toxic beef and beef-that-isn't-beef problem.

It's rarely one big thing that does in the big brand—or even the small business.

It's more death by a thousand tiny cuts, a bleeding in droplets, not gushing flow.

In my book, *No B.S. Guide to Ruthless Management of People and Profits*, I lay out many of these cuts, most self-inflicted wounds, that slowly bleed a business of its reputation and influence, its strength and resilience, and its economic power. In it I refer to a terrific book, *Broken Windows, Broken Business* by Michael Levine, based on the Guiliani turnaround of New York City from crime-riddled garbage dump to newly hospitable city and restored mecca for tourists. If you want to support and safeguard a good brand and the profitable business attached to it, both these books are must-reading. And they are not to be confused with the entire genre of quality and excellence books. Most of those are lofty and inspirational, but mostly theoretical and impractical. I won't name names, but you've probably read a few. The most famous elder of that breed embarrassngly features quite a few brand companies crowned by its author as excellent that are now extinct. The newer, popular entries in this field are loaded with happy talk, mission statements, and team-building psycho-babble. If you want quotes for wall posters, they're dandy. But the protection of a brand from 1,000 cuts is hard-nosed, tough-minded business. My book and Levine's are hard-nosed and tough-minded.

Forgetting What "Brung" You to the Party

There is a line in the song "Luck Be A Lady," popularly sung by Sinatra: ". . . a lady doesn't wander all over the place, blowin' on some other guy's dice." But the world is full of ladies who aren't and gentlemen who aren't and foolish entrepreneurs who do just that. They are invited and brought to the party or game by one escort, but leave him or her standing alone in the corner holding two martinis when their eye is attracted by a sleeker, shinier, sexier siren strolling by.

That graveyard I mentioned, the one over-full with once mighty brands, has a big section of the dead who are there because they forgot or turned their backs on what made them mighty in the first place: direct-response marketing.

A friend of mine once wrote all the copy for a series of full-page and two-page newspaper and magazine ads for an upstart weight-loss product company. The ads rapidly raised the company from obscurity to, at first, profit via direct to consumer selling, but soon also having its key products sold in the biggest chain of health-food stores, discount stores, drugstores, and countless catalogs. Sales soared through millions to tens of millions of dollars, with hundreds of millions in sight. The Wall Street crowd of go-public promoters, investment bankers, and private equity fund vultures began circling. Madison Avenue ad agency rainmakers came calling. The owners were wined and dined, and ever so gently but firmly shamed for their tabloid-style, sensationalist, P.T. Barnum-esque direct -response advertising. Soon, they called my friend the direct-response copywriting wizard to a meeting of the minds at the mansion in the Hamptons, organized something like an intervention for a drug addict. He was surrounded and told that the time had come in the company's maturation to tone down its flashy dress and unrefined used-car sales-like patter and become just a bit more image-conscious and professional in its advertising, in order to safeguard the now prominent brand. He was asked to make only a few changes—like giving up a huge amount of space in the ads to the logo and slogan; replacing the benefit headlines with the company name; dialing back the aggressiveness of the copy; replacing the soap opera celebrity with a white-coated doctor; and replacing the dramatic before and after photos with new "lifestyle photos." Oh, and removing the butt ugly coupon at bottom right. It would be ever so nice, though, if he could sustain the financial performance of the ads. He said only two words, one of which shouldn't be repeated in polite company. And walked away from about $50,000.00 a month in royalties.

The company then moved from one fancy-pants ad agency to the next, each doing more damage than their predecessor. Soon the company was sold, then sold again, for less each time. Its products disappeared from shelves. It no longer exists. A big brand in the making, briefly one of the best known, most popular brands in diet products, soared too close to the image sensitivity sun and then crashed to earth, dust back to dust, and is no more. If I named it you wouldn't even know it.

I have seen this disaster film replayed hundreds of times, by small and large companies in many fields, and I've had my own experiences much like those of my copywriter friend with a number of clients in the big, dumb company category. There is a very famous domain name registry and services company that built its brand with the jet fuel of super-sexy, scandalous Super Bowl commercials that is in the throes of this crash to earth by plucking its own feathers as we speak. I saw its founder interviewed on a financial news network, bravely defending the new guardians of his brand to whom he'd sold the majority of the company and their decision to scale back on the scantily clad babes and sexual innuendo in favor of a more professional approach befitting a company to be taken seriously. I could see his heart wasn't in it. I hope he got paid in cash, not stock. The end is predictable, and it won't be pretty.

It's important to remember that the further away from the building of businesses you get, the higher up the floor numbers you get in the Wall Street towers, the more names there are on the ad agencies' doors, and the more peer awards there are on their walls, the less anybody knows about direct response. They all have opinions—but they rarely have facts. When ad man David Ogilvy said that only *those* direct-response people really *know* what they're doing, he wasn't kidding.

As your business grows and your brand shines brighter, you, too, will find yourself surrounded and romanced by the sleeker, shinier, sexier sirens, the seemingly smarter and more sophisticated professionals. Don't forget who brung you to the dance.

CHAPTER 20

Building a
PERSONAL Brand

by Dan S. Kennedy

O ne of the best current examples of brilliant
personal branding is the country-western personality
Toby Keith, ranked as one of the 100 richest celebrities
by *Forbes* on their 2013 list. Many of the facts about him and his
business used here come from the July 15, 2013, *"Celebrity 100"*
issue of *Forbes.* Keith's career earnings have surpassed $500
million. Over the past five years, he's never earned less than
$48 million. He is but one man. And his market is smaller than
you might think. Country music accounts for less than 15% of
the national radio audience, and it is concentrated in a limited
geographic area. Rather than trying to achieve broader appeal,

Keith has very deliberately sought maximum leverage within a customer base that can be exceptionally loyal and supportive.

Here are some of the important Keith strategies, in addition to having identified a valuable target market and made himself and his brand a perfect match with it. They're not in any particular priority. They're all important.

Synergy, Synergy, Synergy

Every live Toby Keith concert is not only an exercise in brand reinforcement, it is an epic infomercial for his own sponsors and products, with everything artfully integrated. To his hit song "American Ride," he drives onto the stage in a big Ford pickup truck—part of a multimillion-dollar commercial endorsement deal with Ford. His drink of choice is his own brand of tequila with a worm in every bottle, Wild Shot. When he plays "I Love This Bar," it celebrates his restaurant chain named after it. A beloved, popular, or trusted brand, global or local, always has plentiful opportunities for synergy because its customers have multiple needs and desires. The same homeowner who hires a carpet cleaning company probably needs landscaping and lawn care, gutter cleaning, maid service, and auto detailing. You don't have to necessarily be in all those businesses to put them under your brand via joint ventures and strategic alliances, but what I teach in The *No B.S. Business Success* book as "the mini-conglomerate theory" certainly applies. Sponsorship money or barter is often neglected but available to all kinds of businesses.

At GKIC, a multiuse, sequential use synergy is often utilized—for example, the featured speaker at one of our major conferences will provide other content in advance of that appearance for newsletters and tele-seminars; the presentation itself will be recorded and used afterward as a webcast or

DVD to sell an information product built around that speaker. One-time-only seminars beget information products with a long life in catalogs. My book *No B.S. Guide to Marketing to the Affluent* fed a special live training event on the same subject, which birthed an info-product that has been popular for years and a newsletter, *The No B.S. Marketing to the Affluent Letter*, which all GKIC Diamond Members get. I'm big on one thing leading to the next, and it to the next. We could also be more of a mini-conglomerate encompassing more product categories. It's never risen from the back-room "idea board" to priority, but, for example, I've long thought of having my own brand of specially formulated nutritional supplements for brain function and for energy, incorporating the ones I cobble together now. That would be a logical extension of my brand to products people would want. By the way, not only is GKIC Membership useful to you from a training, coaching, networking, and support standpoint, but an added benefit is being able to closely observe and monitor how we market it, and thus borrow our best strategies. You can start free at page 261.

Platform Power

Given a large and loyal audience, Keith has a platform to promote others as well as himself, so why be all about one man? He owns a piece of the quickly made star Taylor Swift. Every time there's a Taylor Swift music CD or download, concert ticket, T-shirt sold, or endorsement deal made, Toby pockets an override. Her recent five years' earnings nearly match his, less, of course, his share. He also owns a piece of the recording company that has Swift, Tim McGraw, and Rascal Flats. His fast-growing chain of restaurants is organized to provide a 20-to-30-city tour for any rising star he takes on. There, of course, it's his Wild Shot that's the drink of choice.

Many business owners, entrepreneurs, authors, and others have platform power that they don't duly appreciate or value, that can be used to aid, promote, and lift others—whether for outright compensation, which I often refer to as "toll position income," or for quid pro quo, reciprocal cross-promotion, or as pay-it-forward investment, or even just because the opportunity to be helpful exists with no harm, foul, or cost. Maybe an investment in karma. I'm frankly very pleased with myself that I've long done this, done it more and more as my own star has risen higher and my influence grown greater, and never worry about creating competition or trading away dollars or any similar miserly concerns.

Ownership and Control

Early on, while still struggling, Keith replaced his band with musicians happy to play for a set salary rather than a share of the take. This and his other ownership moves, like owning the record label, have given him total control over his brand. When his first restaurant opened and he found they had drifted "gourmet" from his prescribed meal items, he stomped his foot and quickly got his way. His preferred fried bologna sandwich, which the suits had removed from the menu, is the chain's number-one bestseller. By owning all or part of everything attached to his brand, he can control the use of the brand and prevent or fix mistakes made by others. It is inevitable that the visionary and personality who builds the brand and its following is judged at some point as having gone as far as he can go with his limited education or sophistication, and newly imported or hired professionals and experts know better. As a company grows, the cries for "professional management" intensify. What happened to his bologna sandwich often happens on a grander scale. No less than Steve Jobs was fired and thrown out of the company he built, only to later be brought back in, with considerable brand damage to repair. Howard Schultz, similar story, with Starbucks. Had he not returned, complete collapse was on the horizon.

You will be challenged about your beliefs about your brand and about your marketing more and more vehemently the more successful you become. You might logically expect the opposite, but you'll be unpleasantly surprised. In my consulting work, I strive to be very careful and thorough in unearthing what makes my client and his relationship with his customers tick, why people have been attracted, what's in the sauce that is invisible to the naked eye and may not be discovered by casual tasting. I am cautious about altering or abandoning what's working, preferring "plus-ing" as Walt Disney called it. Few outside experts or new investors or hired executives are as cautious and considerate. Most are over-eager for change for the sake of change. Many have big but fragile egos and a driving need to demonstrate their cleverness and exert their power as personal validation, not as practical contribution to greater success. Most ask too few questions and are in too much of a hurry to learn about the past or present before making the future. Never, never, never let yourself be intimidated by these people, even though you may need them. Keep my friend Bill Brooks' definition of an expert consultant in mind: a man who knows 365 sexual positions but can't get a date all year. You can't be stupid-stubborn and totally closed-minded, but you don't want to be intimidated or pushed around either. Nobody will be as committed to protecting your brand as you should be.

It's very hard to protect a brand you don't own and own its chief uses. I know this firsthand because I have not owned my brands for a number of years now, and I've had working relationships post-sale with two different owners and companies and three different corporate CEOs, as well as four different book publishers. Such relationships are, I imagine, similar to a man of no means of his own married to a very rich wife. Battles must be chosen judiciously. You can't go to war over every little thing. Compromises, even sacrifices, are required. This is a trade-off you may very well choose to make, just as I did, for my reasons or for other reasons, at some point with your businesses and your brand. If and when you do, try to get as much as you can while giving up as little control as you can, and know that the devil is in the details. I have managed to co-exist with two different owners for nearly 15 years without developing an ulcer, having a heart attack, committing murder, being fired, or being murdered, and with the brands I handed over alive and in reasonably good health. Not all entrepreneurs can do that, nor is it in every entrepreneur's best interests. Just because somebody's standing there with a check doesn't mean you have to take it. One reason not to is the deep emotional connection to your brand as if birthed from your womb and raised by your own breast milk, and feeling it is fragile and vulnerable, so that any and every change made to it or the businesses attached to it feel like personal wounds. I happen to have a knack—a blessing and a curse—for emotional distance and compartmentalization.

My guess, and it is only a guess, is that at some point, probably sooner than later, within years not decades, Toby Keith will wind up selling his entire business, copyrights, and intellectual properties and letting his name, face, personal brand, and brands be used right along with it, while he retires, plays golf even more than now, and does other things unrelated to the entertainment business. If and when he does, the brand will be used in ways he's happy about and ways he's unhappy about, and he'll have forfeited his say-so. But that kind of equity and exit is one of the reasons to build a brand.

Polarization

Toby Keith's hit songs' lyrics have consistently been jingoistic, reflecting right-wing extremes, patriotic themes, and military support. He is the son of a military veteran who never shies from flag-waving. The hit song he put out shortly after the first September 11 Attack Day (NYC, not the more recent Benghazi), titled "Courtesy of the Red, White and Blue," includes this line: "We'll put a boot in your ass. It's the American Way." He is perfectly happy offending with such material, and responding should someone pick a fight over it. Natalie Maines of the Dixie Chicks called the song "ignorant," and Keith responded by displaying a made-up family photo of her and Saddam Hussein as a giant backdrop at his concerts.

I have plenty of liberals in my fan base, in GKIC Membership, and in various relationships. I do pro bono work for the Cleveland Food Bank and for Happy Trails Farm Animal Sanctuary, both run by liberals. My mystery novel co-author Les Roberts (book title: *Win, Place or Die*) is a blue-collar liberal who reminds me of Studs Terkel, *and* he's a recently converted vegan. Still, my conservative/libertarian politics are very clear in my written works and speeches and seminars. And I have not held back my ire and disgust for President Obama. The majority of my audience of small-business owners, entrepreneurs, and self-employed professionals skews conservative, at least fiscally if not socially. So I do tread relatively safe ground with most, strongly resonate with many, but undoubtedly offend some who must look past these positions of mine to otherwise benefit—and most importantly, I repel many.

Deliberately repelling people from a brand is a more common practice than many realize. The CEO of Abercrombie & Fitch made headlines and sparked controversy and criticism by perhaps ill-advisedly detailing who he did not want patronizing their stores or ever seen wearing their apparel, and how he deliberately directed everything from store design to advertising to sizes of clothes stocked to clearly and adamantly tell those people they are not welcome. A & F is a valuable and powerful retail brand, with a lot of its value tied to an aura of exclusivity. There was a lot of expressed shock by pundits over his statements about this, but I was not surprised one bit.

I believe that a price tag attached to power is polarization. Vanilla is only a successful position for ice cream.

Prolific Output

Beginning back in 1993, Toby Keith released at least one new album every year through the year 2000, selling, on average, about 500,000 copies. His 1999 album sold 3.1 million copies. If you want a vibrant brand and brand loyalist population, I do not think you have any choice but to be extremely prolific. You must bring a lot of "new" to the table, frequently. You need constant communication—at GKIC, Diamond Members are "touched" one way or another by me at least 112 times during a calendar year, by GKIC itself above that at least another 100 times, and they see me in person at two national conferences and at least one special event. In total, we're achieving near daily connection. I also strive for omnipresence, meaning every time you turn around in a complete circle in your environment or in your industry, you see, hear, hear about, or somehow bump into me. Just as Toby Keith wants his brand of booze on the bar in your man-cave, his endorsed pickup truck in your garage, his CDs playing in it when you drive it, I want my Dan Kennedy bobble-head, posters, and books in your office, my CDs playing in your car, and No B.S. logo apparel in your closet and on your back. This is a strategy I learned studying Disney.

Even true-blue brand loyalists and longtime fans are increasingly easily distracted. They are under bombardment by seductions every minute in every media. "Brand loyalist" is really an antiquated word still used by all the brand academics, theorists, and agencies selling you on brand, and I've used it in this book as a convenience. But the truth is, loyalty is more of an endangered species by the day, and it is very, very dangerous to presume you have any of it, from anybody. The savvier position is that of the paranoid, as I described in Chapter 19. You get up each and every morning assuming your fences dissolved during the night and your entire herd has wandered off in 1,000 different directions, and you must ride hard to catch them, re-entice them to follow you, round 'em all up, put up a new fence, grab a nap, and do it all over again. And, by all means, rely more on real, strong, solid fences than simple loyalty. In direct marketing, we build those, for example, out of membership, continuity or forced continuity with automatic recurring payments, and pain of disconnect ideally more complex than an emotional bond. These are strategies and tactics commonly found in businesses of varied kinds owned by GKIC-trained operators and entrepreneurs that you rarely find in the same kind of businesses absent GKIC influence.

Work

There's a dirty word. People who build and sustain valuable personal brands work a lot and work at it a lot. The $1 million or so Toby Keith pulls out of a concert is pale in comparison to the other revenues of his personal empire, but he is nonetheless out there in person, on the plane, then on the bus, then on the stage, doing manual labor, being seen, pressing the flesh. Beyond that, he is writing songs; recording, finding, signing, and promoting other stars; doing deals; visiting restaurants; *working*. The "escape from work" attitude and delusion that has permeated society as a whole and, more troubling, the business and entrepreneur community to a far, far greater extent post-internet than pre-internet, and even more so in very recent years, is a vile, evil cancer destructive to the American and world economies; to individuals' mental, emotional, and physical health; and to society as a whole.

I do not begrudge Tim Ferris's phenomenal success with his original book titled *The 4 Hour Workweek*, nor with the 4-Hour brand he has built behind it. The content of the original book is better and more honest than its title, picked by popular preference via a Google AdWords test-marketing campaign. Tim has said complimentary things about me, and I certainly respect him. *But.* The very fact that this was the popular and successful title and that people would actually lust after and believe in the idea of grand success and four hours of work per week speaks volumes about the stupid sloth of the public. It's not new. There was, decades ago, a huge seller titled *The Lazy Man's Way to Riches*. But even it didn't dare to say *The Lazy Man's Way to Riches With Just 4 Hours of Work Per Week*. And now it's worse. It's shameful. It makes me embarrassed for my fellow creatures walking upright.

If you closely follow the real schedules, activities, and disciplines of virtually any or every highly successful person, particularly one building or sustaining a valuable personal brand, you won't find a four-hour week; you will find them doing a whole lot of work, out in public, and behind closed doors in private.

I'll quickly mention another entertainer who has built an incredible personal brand, Lady Gaga. If you don't even know who she is, it's perfectly okay. I have very smart and aware clients who only very recently discovered her existence and, predictably, found her bizarre. But you might very well want to study her, and a book worth reading is *Monster Loyalty: How Lady Gaga Turns Followers into Fanatics* by Jackie Huba. A few takeways: While she has talent and has invested a lot of time and work in developing it, she freely admits she's far from the best singer out there. She is well aware that her openly expressed political and societal opinions are polarizing, but she defines her number-one job as playing to her fan base, and specifically to the top 1% of her fan base, those who buy everything and follow her obsessively, whom she calls her Monsters. She is more interested in keeping her current customers than attracting new ones, and she is not at all concerned with converting people who don't understand her. One of her favorite quotes is, "If you are not pissing someone off, you are not doing your job." That's very close to a principle I've long taught, expressed: If you haven't pissed off somebody by noon, you're under quota. Get busy. Lady Gaga's revenues exceed those of Toby Keith, by the way.

And What If You Have a Tired Brand?

It is relatively common for a good personal brand, and an entertainer, author, other celebrity, expert, or an entire company to outlive its productive, profitable customer base. It is even more common for a good brand to fatigue, to feel "been there, done that," and lose its following to an inferior but newer person, place, or product.

In the 2000s, the famous singer Tony Bennett was a tired brand. If you don't know him for anything else, you might click with his most famous song, *I Left My Heart In San Francisco*. He is of The Rat Pack era, but has outlived all of them and is still performing, recording, and newly popular as I write this. His son Danny reinvigorated Bennett with a marketing strategy known as co-branding. You might be familiar with it thanks to Doritors tacos at Taco Bell, Jim Beam Bourbon enhanced steakburgers at T.G.I.F.'s, or other food co-brands. Ford has a King's Ranch truck. Bennett was paired with the just-mentioned Lady Gaga, Carrie Underwood, and other very contemporary singers in a series of *Duets* albums that brought him to the attention of an entire generation of fans who would otherwise have ignored him. The strategy was stolen directly from Frank Sinatra, who did it with two of his own *Duets* albums in the 1990s.

This was a double dose of new life for the tired Tony Bennett brand. First, same brand, same personality, same songs—to an entirely new audience, surprised to find themselves appreciative of their new discovery. Second, same brand attached to other, newer, hotter, trendier brands, making the old one seem and feel reborn as new, too.

Let's Not Forget: Personal Brand-Building by DIRECT RESPONSE

Toby Keith originally built his brand by direct selling of concert tickets and the manual labor of performing. In fact, he built a fan/customer base to make money day-to-day, while building his brand that could be leveraged far beyond the stage. I built my brand and brand equity predominately with 15 years of intense travel speaking 70 to 80 times a year, accompanied by direct-response advertising in magazines, direct mail, article placement in media, and other direct-response marketing. I built a fan/customer base to make money day to day, while building a brand that could be leveraged far beyond the stage. I have now routinely taken successful business owners in different niches and rapidly made them famous names and known brands in those niches entirely through direct-response advertising.

I have always told my peers in professional speaking, and told authors, that the nifty trick is to avoid going broke while you're busy getting rich and famous. Personal brand-building by direct response makes that trick possible.

CHAPTER 21

The Brand No One Believed In

Exclusive Interview with MARK VICTOR HANSEN,
Co-Creator of *Chicken Soup for the Soul*
by Dan S. Kennedy

D AN: Mark, we're going to talk about the Chicken *Soup for the Soul* books, publishing empire, brand, and brand-licensing business. I want to acknowledge that you've also built a very good personal brand for yourself, and if people aren't aware, you're the author of a number of other books, you've had a long and very successful speaking career, and you're involved in all sorts of entrepreneurial ventures. People can visit www.MarkVictorHansen.com. With *Chicken Soup for the Soul*, you and Jack Canfield built one of the biggest, if not the biggest and best-known brand on the nonfiction side of publishing, starting with nothing more than the idea and determination. I want to look at the brand-building, from the beginning to the present. We can start with the start.

MVH: Jack Canfield and I were both speaking at the Mandela Conference. There were 6,000 people there. Jack and I were both breakout session speakers. He sat in on my presentation. I think there were 600 or 700 there. When I was done, he asked to take me to lunch. We swapped stories and befriended each other. I think we each saw something in the other person. Jack is a really brilliant Harvard guy. We started talking regularly on the phone. We met up again some months later. He told me he was thinking of doing a book of stories—I think he called them happy little stories. He said, "I've got 63." I said, "A lot of them are mine!—that I shared with you. I think we should do this together." So we started working on this thing. Of course, at the start we were both just thinking book, not brand. But pretty early on, I started seeing this in a bigger way.

DAN: I'd like to point out that this *isn't* a particularly amazing origin story. Two speakers working in the same subject categories meet, bond, start brainstorming, and agree to work on a book of inspirational stories. What a lot of people don't get about success is that starting and doing something, anything, can lead to great things. Not starting can't lead anywhere.

MVH: Well, here's where that led: in June 2013, we came out with the 20th Anniversary Edition of the first, original *Chicken Soup for the Soul* book. My story is the lead story. Jack wrote the preface, which tells this just as I did. In total, there have been more than *half a billion Chicken Soup for the Soul* books sold worldwide. Anyway, we went to work, and it took us three years to put that first collection of stories together. Then we went to the publishers in New York City to sell it. That didn't go so well. As you know, 144 publishers turned us down. One hundred and forty-four nos. Our agent fired us. I still have his signed letter in my office, telling me that this book will never sell. Jack and I put three-ring notebooks in our backpacks and went to the big book publishing industry convention, and pitched publishers ourselves. At the very end, we connected with the owner of what was then a very small publishing house, HCI, Health Communications Inc. They had only published a couple books successfully, and they were in the hole financially, but we didn't know it. The publisher, Peter Vegso, said, "We'll publish it if you'll guarantee to buy 20,000 copies at $6.00 each." It cost about 50 cents to print, and we're paying six dollars. But we had a publisher.

DAN: Joan Rivers has this line: walk through *any* door. By the way, I got my first book deal exactly the same way you did—on the convention floor, accosting publishing executives who didn't want to talk to me. I finally connected with the president of a small Canadian publisher and made a deal. And I had to first write books they wanted as a contract author before they would publish the one I wanted to do, my original *No B.S. Business Success* book.

In Search of a System

MVH: After 144 rejections, any yes is a good yes. So, Jack and I looked at each other and said, "Now what?" Jack was the creative guy, the writer, the Harvard scholar, and he wasn't sure whether we'd sell one or a million. I said, "Let me do the selling. I've been selling since I was 9 years old." I knew there had to be a system for making a book a big success. I worked for Dr. R. Buckminster Fuller, and he always said everything is a system. That's a big tip for people, about a brand, and about licensing, which has become the business built by the books. *There's a system.* I knew I could figure it out. I learned early, starting with speaking, at the National Speakers Association. When you and I were hanging out there, there were usually only about ten people who were the best in anything. At the time, the book business was a $25 billion business, with a lot of personal growth type of authors. So I made up my list of the best of those, the most successful of those, and went around and personally interviewed them— Scott Peck, Wayne Dyer, Barbara DeAngelis, John Gray, a number of others. I didn't ask about writing—I can write, and Jack is the finest editor on planet earth. I wanted to know: *How do you promote, market, and sell books?* Scott Peck had a number-one book for 12 years that made $40 million. *I wanted to know what he was doing that nobody else was.* We got something from each person, and mostly, something different from each person. We had each suggestion on a sticky note and wound up with 1,094 of them all over a wall in Jack's office. We kept shuffling them, until we had a business plan. The way I laid it out, we'd sell 1 million, then 10 million books. We'd do $5 million, $10 million, $50 million. I had these crazy goals, but I also knew what had to be done to achieve them, so they weren't *that* crazy.

DAN: I just want to emphasize that point. You just described a process that anyone could do but hardly anybody does. Very few people are really determined and dogged about getting the information they need. You did your homework. You gathered information. You kind of made a pest of yourself to get it—which, by the way, you are very good at. I tell people all the time that nobody is better at what I call

"The Ask" than Mark Victor Hansen. You prepared. You also got started moving forward, taking action. I suppose your book, your Chicken Soup idea could be called The Brand Nobody Believed In. But you did, with good reason, because you put together information that led to a plan you could believe in.

MVH: That's what makes crazy big goals realistic. People are always trying to shrink others' ambitions, telling them they have to set more realistic goals. It's not the goal that's the problem. It's the lack of a realistic plan. So, here we are. We've sold half a billion books, with 300 million of those in China, which is interesting. According to the people at *Guinness Book of World Records*, nobody's done that. And I want to be the first guy to sell a billion books.

DAN: I would not bet against you. And I want people to grasp the amazing nature of what you've accomplished, just on the publishing side. Big brands are rare in the book business, particularly on the non-fiction side. In fiction, there are character brands—for kids, for example, you can go back to *The Hardy Boys* and *Nancy Drew*, Baum's Oz series, and come forward to *Harry Potter*. On the non-fiction side, you have established brands that come to books, like Betty Crocker® or Weight Watchers®, You have a few business niche series, like Levinson's Guerrilla Marketing or my No B.S.-branded series. Maybe the biggest broad one is the *For Dummies* brand. But you spread Chicken Soup very wide, touching every kind of person: mothers, fathers, military veterans, every niche. The number of titles is dizzying. And, really, the success of the books is just the beginning. So, let's stay on track. You've put together a plan out of collected tips and Post-it Notes®. Now what?

MVH: The publisher wasn't going to do anything but publish—and push those 20,000 books on us. Jack and I scraped up about $180,000.00 for promotion. We tried several different publicists, but I kept trying to connect with the best, Arielle Ford. She was working with the biggest authors in this area. I finally got to her by calling a friend of mine, an author, who knew her, Dr. Harold Bloomfield, and I asked him to tell me what her biggest challenge was, what she had a shortage of and a need for. He said: time. Now I called her and, instead of trying to sell her on representing us, I said, "Look, you need time. When I was in graduate school with Bucky Fuller, he taught us how to expand time. I can solve your problem for you. You can solve a problem for me." That got us Arielle Ford. Then I got us with Rick Frishman, who is the best at booking drive-time radio. I was starting a day of interviews at 3:00 D<small>IP</small> . my time and moving across the country. At one point, we had some luck: Dr. Deepak Chopra got delayed in India and couldn't do a cover story interview for *People* magazine, and Arielle had to replace him. She asked if we were willing to let the reporter basically live with us for a week. Well, we're busy. We're consumed with the books and their promotion, but we're both speaking and earning a living, too, but you make room for opportunity like that.

DAN: I'd call it *earned* luck. And what I want to hear about now is the sacrifice. Here you started with a book, then books, and wound up with a very valuable brand—which we will get to, but I think it's important people understand that such a thing rarely happens without people making very big trade-offs and sacrifices.

MVH: On the front end, the sacrifices are huge. Jack and I sacrificed a lot of income to take time away from the ways we earned income and put that time into writing and promoting these first books. I was personally calling owners of independent bookstores all over the country. Doing radio interviews. We found it literally ate our lives. We quickly figured out we didn't just want a book out of it, some brief fame. So, a second book. Then a third. Our third book was *Chicken Soup for the Teen Soul,* and our publisher predicted a bomb. "I've got teenagers," he said "They buy clothes, music CDs, and concert tickets. They will not buy your book." And we sold 19 million books. I like to say that teenagers talk all the time but don't talk at the *soul-ular* level, and this book opened up those conversations. It also opened up the college speaking circuit for me, and I was quickly getting booked, first at $10,000.00, then at $20,000.00, and talking to 20,000 college kids at a time—because *Chicken Soup for the Soul* was a huge thing. Kids were telling me, "I stayed in college because of you . . . I was so lonely and scared I was going to quit school and go home." Anyway, at certain points, a thing like this picks up speed and begins generating its own momentum. But I'll give you a specific sacrifice story . . . .

DAN: Those college speaking gigs basically gave you book-and-brand promotion opportunities without you dipping into your pocket. I always looked at speaking as an advertising opportunity, and instead of paying to advertise, getting paid *to* advertise. It's important if you're starting this process without access to the gold in Fort Knox to figure something like that out. It's no guarantee of success, but it can be easy to build a brand if you can pour a ton of money into it. Richard Branson said the way to start an airline and become a millionaire is to start with a billion dollars. The focus of this entire book that I'm interviewing you for is brand-building without lots of money to buy it with.

MVH: *We* definitely did *not* have a lot of money. So, this story. Jack and I were traveling, by ourselves, no assistants, and we didn't have a lot of money, so we're staying together in one hotel room, and finally we are going to be on a major NBC show. At the time, we might do a speech or seminar during the day in one city, get on a plane at night, arrive somewhere at 1:00 in the morning and have to get up to do interviews at 6:00 DIP . This time, we had to get up at 4:00 DIP . to be in the NBC studio at 6:00 DIP . And, by the way, when the media hits, they all want you, right now. There were no cell phones then—we were squeezing in phone interviews with rolls of coins in our pockets at pay phones. Anyway, Jack and I get to our hotel room at about 1:00 DIP . and the alarm goes off at 4:00 DIP . I look over, and Jack's gone to sleep in his little three-piece suit and little red tie. I said, "Jack, you've got to get up, we've got to get to the station." He said profane words to me. At the time, *NBC LIVE* was the biggest thing. It's interesting how much has changed in just 20 years. Then, there wasn't the proliferation of media. You had a handful of big shows on networks. It took us five years to get on *Oprah*. People say—didn't Oprah make you? No, we were a success already. Jack and I probably sacrificed a billion hours of sleep to get everything going to ultimately sell half a billion books. At least it felt that way. We were starting this fire by rubbing sticks together. We were exhausted most of the time. We over-ate and ate for energy. There was no time to exercise. It was a blur of book signings, interviews, speeches, travel. It takes a lot to build momentum. Then, like Napoleon Hill said in *Think And Grow Rich*, when riches begin to come, they come in such an avalanche and overflowing abundance, you wonder where they've been hiding all of the lean years. I know you've had that experience. We certainly had it.

DAN: I have on several occasions—and teach it as "The Phenomenon®," the time in your life when you suddenly accomplish more in one year than in the previous ten years. When it happens, it happens for a reason. People can learn from you and me how to trigger and accelerate The Phenomenon®.

Anyway, the story. At this point, you've hit, you've got one book after another coming out of your story factory, you and Jack are in demand by the media and as speakers. Now, let's leap from the books to the brand built by the books—and that is vital to get. You didn't invest in brand-building per se. You didn't even start with that as a clear intention. This brand was built by the selling of books. But let's get into its value . . . .

Beyond the Original, Core Business to the Even Bigger Opportunity

MVH: As you know, I'm a voracious reader. I've probably read over 5,000 autobiographies and biographies. I read every one of your books. One of the things I'm reading for is *opportunity*. I was reading two books, one on Spielberg and one on Lucas. Both made a lot of money with movies—and we're working on a *Chicken Soup* movie. *E.T.* made $800 million for Spielberg. A "feel good" movie, by the way. But his licensing made $1.5 billion. I ran into Jack's office and said, "We have to stop thinking like publishers. We've got to get into licensing." Jack said, "What do you know about licensing?" Well, I didn't know anything about publishing or creating bestsellers when we started. I was confident there was a system for this somewhere. We could create a plan. Licensing was a $135 billion business in America. It may have begun with Walt Disney. And what's so fantastic about licensing a brand is that not only do you make money from the licensing, but all the licensed products and promotions keep building the brand and making it more valuable so you can do more licensing for more money. That *is* Disney. So, that day, we got into the brand-licensing business.

We found the big trade show of the licensing industry. The association. We found the top licensing agent and got her on board. We did a lot of licenses in a hurry, pretty indiscriminately. Even some little licensing deals made money. Jack and I wrote *Chicken Soup for the Soul Conversation Starter Cards,* with a question on each card, deep, soul-searching questions. We sold the rights to that for $650,000.00. We got better and better at this. After we did the book *Chicken Soup for the Pet Lover's Soul,* with Jay Leno, and Dr. Marty Becker, one of the world's top veterinarians, we almost did a licensing deal with Purina, but they were actually having trouble with dogs not liking their new products. I wound up making a deal with Diamond Pet Foods, and we've got *Chicken Soup for the Soul* branded healthy, organic, outstanding dog food. We just started, in 2,700 supermarkets. When we sold the entire *Chicken Soup* brand, and I re-committed and stayed involved, the new owners came in with an even bigger brand expansion vision, and contacts and capabilities. We had a relationship with Campbell's before, and did promotions, like putting three *Chicken Soup for the Soul* stories inside their labels, and that sold a lot of books. With Nora Roberts' *Chicken Soup for the Romantic Soul,* we did it with Diet Coke® for six months. But I always thought we should really be in business with Campbell's Soup, and the new folks running the brand licensing got that done. Now we've got *Chicken Soup for the Soul* soups and sauces and condiments. The man helming this is Bill Rouhana. He's not very public. He likes being a behind-the-scenes dealmaker. His background as an entrepreneur and investor is incredible. He's convinced that in two or three years the *Chicken Soup for the Soul* brand will be even better known, bigger, and more valuable with foods than it has been with books.

I can believe that's right. We're also working on a movie, with the company created by the founder of Federal Express, Fred Smith. They did *Blindside* with Sandra Bullock. The producer involved was responsible for *Fried Green Tomatoes,* and it made $360 million. I'm seeing us as having the feel-good, holiday movie of 2014.

How to Think Bigger than the Other Guy

DAN: People reading this may be gasping for breath, and might disqualify themselves. Somebody reading this has a local shop, a great local restaurant, he's a dentist in Spokane, he's a stockbroker in New York. Whatever. He says, "Really, me?"

MVH: You and I have known each other and been friends for about 40 years. We've both run through our share of skeptics and critics. I've been accused of a lot of things, but one that I'm never accused of is *small* thinking. You've got to have a big dream, a magnificent obsession that absorbs you. Jack and I said that we want to change the whole world, one story at a time. We figured out what was needed for that: stories that created goose bumps, God bumps, make you weak in the knees, made you cry, feel joy, feel hope. We owned that idea, and it owned us. *Anybody can do this*—find or create something they can get excited about and committed to and believe in, and that can build their business and build a brand or provide the business and brand-building opportunity.

Then you've got to build a team. At first it was just Jack and me. When everybody else is telling you to forget it, you need somebody other than yourself saying we're going to do this. I was even under attack by my own spouse; she was saying, "You spend more time with Jack than you do with me." We worked at getting others to join the team, to contribute, to open doors for us. You can't motivate big people with small ideas. To build a great team you need great ideas. I happen to believe there's a very big opportunity inside every little business and every person, waiting to be let out. There was a Nightingale-Conant audio program that I created with a title "How to Think Bigger than You Ever Thought You Could Think."

You also have to think differently. One of my daughters recently graduated cum laude, and at the graduation, the speaker was talking about all the change that's happened during the five years those kids went through school. Five years back, 98% of communication was talk, on the phone—now it's text on the phone. Blockbuster was big. Now they're gone, and Netflix is big. He went through a whole list, and what they all had in common was *disruptive innovation* and *disruptive marketing.* That's what we did, a lot, with *Chicken Soup for the Soul.* We created an innovation in creating and assembling content and involving co-authors and partners so that we could put out a huge number of book titles at high speed and dominate a market. We built a brand, and we have done a lot of licensing with it by bringing innovative ideas to different kinds of companies—not here's a brand, pay us, but here's a great idea for you to use our brand, for us to do something unique together.

Bill Rouhana, who bought our company, said he was buying it because there is so much noise and there's going to be so much more noise in the future that the only thing people are going to be able to do to make decisions is to trust a brand—and everybody knows our brand. I do a whole talk on this I call *"Brand to Command."* It's really about identity, visibility, familiarity, and conformity. They all bought Mustangs together because when Iacocca was at Ford, he made that the brand, he convinced everybody it was the cool car. Then they all bought vans together, because they all had little kids together. What will they all buy or do together next? Will they all buy Teslas together? They are always all doing something together. Great brands have the power to command. Bill thinks, we think, we've got that kind of a brand. We've done it with the books—we made buying different, specific *Chicken Soup for the Soul* books as gifts for mothers, fathers, sons, daughters, the grieving, the romantic, the pet owner, the you-name-it, the thing they all did together. An entire generation has done this together. Now we'll see just how much farther we can take our brand.

The "Secret" of *Chicken Soup for the Soul's* Appeal

DAN: We can't exit this without getting to the crux of your brand's appeal. Why do you think it caught on and became as big as it has and has the longevity it has had?

MVH: Everybody was already familiar with what chicken soup means. It means you're safe and cared for and getting something good, that's good for you, that heals. And everybody wants to be reached and touched and healed at the *soul-ular* level. The stories Jack and I chose for all the books are all high impact, very authentic, and insightful. I've actually had 20,000 stories memorized, stories for any and every occasion. Storytelling, as you know, is incredibly powerful. We created something that people responded to, but nobody should ever think it caught on and took off on its own or by some single stroke of luck or one big media break or anything like that.

DAN: Mark, thank you, thank you, and thank you for a great interview.

MARK VICTOR HANSEN is the author of a diverse collection of books including *One-Minute Millionaire*, *The Aladdin Factor*, and his most recent, *UR The Solution*. He is the recipient of numerous awards, including The Horatio Alger Award from the Horatio Alger Association of Distinguished Americans, and he is known as a passionate humanitarian, working for organizations such as Habitat for Humanity, the American Red Cross, March of Dimes, and Childhelp USA. Mark receives extensive media coverage, in *Time*, *U.S. News & World Report*, *USA Today*, *The New York Times*, and *Entrepreneur*, and on TV, on *Oprah*, *CNN*, and *The Today Show*. As one of the most sought-after and popular professional speakers of our time, Mark has beneficially altered the thinking and touched the hearts of more than 6,000 audiences worldwide. He is available for a limited number of speaking engagements, coaching, and consulting engagements and interesting projects. www.MarkVictorHansen.com.

Lost in Space

by Dan S. Kennedy

I grew up watching the black-and-white TV show *Lost in Space*. As I recall, it was the old Swiss Family Robinson relocated into a space capsule that had somehow lost the ability to get back to earth, and just drifted from planet to planet, place to place, misadventure to misadventure. No one on earth even knew they were out there. Despite the fact that they very definitely existed, they were as a practical matter invisible.

Today's entrepreneur is very easily lost in space; so is today's consumer. There are, as of this writing, 55,000 YouTube channels. The number of individual videos on YouTube is a fast-multiplying multiple of that. Consider that as a representative of the epic media problem facing every entrepreneur. Look at the number of titles of books in any category at Amazon, the number of answers to a term searched at Google, the number of emails in an in-box, the number of competing car commercials in just the same hour of prime-time TV or a TV newscast, the number of competing ads in a magazine, and the number of magazines at a Barnes and Noble newsstand. If you mail to known responders to direct mail, which you want to do, and you could see the quantity of catalogs, magalogs, and solo direct-mail pieces in a week of their mail, you'd fear for forests.

There are so many choices in virtually every category of commerce it's dizzying. I'm only 58 years old; I'm not yet, exactly, an aged dinosaur. But when I became an adult, you still got local telephone service from the phone company and you got long-distance services from AT&T. Today, many competitors with many price plans are selling in their own stores but also at Best Buy, Walmart, and, of course, online. The dairy section at the supermarket is the fastest expanding area, with a myriad of choices for milk and milk alternatives made from soy and almonds and Martian grass, yogurts, and yogurt alternatives, infused with healthy probiotics—but there are different strains and kinds of those, no sugar added, sugar free, low fat, low calorie, organic.

Few consumers can actually start from scratch with most purchasing decisions. Who has time to carefully investigate every phone plan? To go to the grocery store with a blank mind and compare every label for every type of food you want?

There are solutions for the marketer, and this book has presented many, and the many organized into one approach. I hope you will go back through the book a second, even third time, and discuss it with your advisors or team. Brand is a solution. Brand is what consumers use as a shortcut, so they are not, themselves, lost in space. Facing the wide array of yogurts spread over many shelves, many consumers ignore everything but one brand they know, like Dannon. That, pardon the expression, freezes every other producer's yogurt out. Of course, if their eye is caught by another brand or co-brand, like Weight Watchers yogurt or Starbucks yogurt or Arthritis Foundation-approved yogurt, a competitive battle ensues. Other consumers may take their shortcut by price, first by being at Walmart instead of Whole Foods, but then by the generic brand. But that's why it's important for a specialized yogurt alternative producer, Lifeway, an up-and-coming health food maker I'm watching and have invested in stock in (as of this writing—not that I'm giving investment advice) to have its products at the uppity Whole Foods and at the plebian Walmart, which it does. And to invest in advertising that can build its brand and brand preference with consumers, which I hope they do via direct response.

Which brings us to the second big solution, which is circumvention of search. You can avoid the lost-in-space syndrome if and when you show up alone and show up like no one else. It's vital to understand that more goods and services are sold to people who were not actively looking for and trying to choose between versions of those goods and services than are sold to people already searching and comparing, and this is trebly true when you climb to higher price points, more specialty products, financial services, and investments, as well as more affluent consumers. This is why targeted direct marketing is so important to learn, understand, and use. To that end, I urge starting on that path with my book *No B.S. Guide to DIRECT Marketing for NON-Direct Marketing Businesses (2nd Edition)*.

I do *not* want you to underestimate the importance and power of circumventing search. You need strategies to be with your potential customer *before* he goes to Google or Yelp or the Yellow Pages or Amazon or anywhere else looking for a solution to a problem you solve or desire you meet. That does not necessarily mean you don't utilize search-driven marketing, with online search engines, and social media, as well as good, old, still-very-effective (in many categories) search media like the Yellow Pages and association, industry, or consumer directories. But if you depend on search activity to feed you, there will always be others stealing the meal right off the table. You will go to sleep every night not knowing if Google will alter its algorithms while you sleep, essentially dropping a nuclear bomb on the road your new customers travel to you on. You will basically be forever in a bidding war for customers. You can easily get lost in that space.

You can never truly control your own destiny. Brand provides a great advantage in search environments, but there is far greater advantage in a marketing system that circumvents search altogether. I have written a very detailed report on this subject titled: *Grow Rich & Stay Rich with Peace of Mind: CIRCUMVENT SEARCH*. You may obtain a copy free of cost or obligation simply by asking me for it directly, via a fax on your business letterhead or with your name, physical address, email address, a note about your type of business, and your "honor system" note that you have purchased at least three copies of this book to gift to business peers, associates, or clients. I promise the report will be worth that favor. And this is the only way to get it. My direct fax number is (602) 269-3113.

Finally, the third solution is customer-get-a-customer or referrals. Word-of-mouth advertising can be expanded exponentially from over-the-backyard fence conversation to easy sharing with hundreds or even thousands of "Friends" by online social media. Consumers escape

being lost in space via three shortcuts through choice: being reached and persuaded directly, one to one, through direct marketing; by brand; and by friend, neighbor, or peer referral, asked for or volunteered. Brand helps this, but so does good direct-response media so there is an effective place for the referror to send the referee. All three connect. To be successful, you need to be effectively using and integrating all three. To that end, I cannot urge you strongly enough to grab the FREE TRIAL OFFER on page 261 and get involved with all of us at and associated with GKIC. GKIC is quite simply the world leader in this integrated marketing approach, made understandable, practical, and usable by businesses of every imaginable breed, type, and size. GKIC provides vital information and practical training, support and coaching, networking and facilitated alliances with like-minded entrepreneurs actively and successfully implementing these strategies, even connections with quality vendors of every service you might need who are particularly knowledgeable in our methods and themselves trained to work with our members. There's just nothing like GKIC.

The space you and your customers find yourselves in is only growing and expanding, so it is getting ever easier to get lost in it. Entirely new spaces within the vast space of the marketing universe keep getting created. Amazon and Facebook are two examples. **It is up to you to connect with your customers, to shine a bright beacon that attracts them and that they can follow to find you in the vast blackness and use to navigate their way through all the clutter, the "space junk," floating around in that vast space.** Here we have given you three powerful beacons. I hope I'll be hearing from you, of your success with them, and even meeting you at a future GKIC event, maybe even crowning you as one of the GKIC Marketers or Entrepreneurs of the Year and inviting you to an all-expenses-paid Winners Weekend. Let this be the Start, not the End, of our work together to build your business, your brand, and your fortune!

About the Authors

D AN S. KENNEDY is a strategic advisor, consultant, business coach, and editor of six business newsletters. He directly influences more than one million small business owners annually, and has a long track record of taking entrepreneurs to seven-figure incomes and multimillionaire wealth. He has also consulted and worked with some of the biggest and fastest growth mainstream and niche brands built by direct response, including Guthy-Renker Corporation's Pro-Activ® (acne products), HealthSource (over 350 chiropractic clinics), Weight Watchers International, Iron Tribe Fitness, and many others. He is also one of the highest compensated direct-response copywriters in the world. As a speaker, he has frequently shared the stage with an eclectic assortment of celebrity entrepreneurs, including Gene Simmons (KISS), Joan Rivers, and Donald Trump; four former U.S. Presidents and other world leaders; celebrated business speakers, including Zig Ziglar, Brian Tracy, Jim Rohn, and Tom Hopkins; and entertainment and sports stars. Dan's own conferences have featured fascinating entrepreneurs and CEOs such as Jim McCann (1-800-Flowers), Nido Qubein (High Point University), and Jake Steinfeld (Body By Jake)—all brand-builders extraordinaire! Dan is also a serial entrepreneur and active investor. His own *NO B.S.* and *RENEGADE MILLIONAIRE* brands are widely recognized throughout the entrepreneurial and marketing communities. Information about his books can be found at www.NoBSBooks.com, his other published work and the membership organization he founded at www.DanKennedy. com, and he can be reached directly regarding interesting speaking, consulting, or copywriting engagements by fax at (602) 269-3113.

JIM CAVALE AND FORREST WALDEN are the entrepreneurs leading Iron Tribe Fitness, the fastest growing limited membership brick-and-mortar location fitness gym franchise network in North America, recognized by *Entrepreneur, The Wall Street Journal*, and *CRM* magazine. Their business model is unique. Their business methods' success is extraordinary. They are also the authors of *Iron Tribe Business*. For more information about or to connect with Jim and Forrest: www.IronTribeFranchise.com/NoBS. Also, if you are interested in owning and/or being an investor in a business with a powerful, valuable brand, in a dynamic growth industry, the Iron Tribe franchise opportunities may be for you. For information go to www.IronTribeFranchise.com.

NICK NANTON AND J.W. DICKS lead The Celebrity Branding Agency. Nick is an Emmy-winning documentary film producer, a gifted and skilled business storyteller, and an exceptionally knowledgeable media insider. Jack Dicks is an entertainment, intellectual property, and franchise attorney; business development consultant; and marketing advisor. They have perfected systems for personal branding that include dramatically accelerated national media exposure and credits. They are also the authors of *Celebrity Branding You: "People Buy People."* For more information about or to connect with Nick and Jack: www.CelebrityBrandingAgency.com.

BILL GOUGH built one of the most successful Allstate® insurance agencies in America, and went on to develop a training, coaching, and consulting program embraced by thousands of his peers. Today, he is the leading marketing and business growth authority in the insurance industry. www. BGIMarketing.com.

STEVE ADAMS operates exceptionally successful retail stores across the country, under the auspices of a national brand, but fueled by direct-response marketing. His retail business can be seen at www.AskPSP.com. He is also involved in e-commerce, information publishing and marketing, and consulting. His book, *The Passionate Entrepreneur,* presents essential, experience-based building blocks for entrepreneurial success and can be found at www.Passionate Entrepreneur.com.

MARK VICTOR HANSEN is the co-creator of and has been the driving marketing force of the *Chicken Soup for the Soul* publishing and licensing empire, begun with one book initially rejected by 144 publishers. He is also the author of a number of success, wealth, and self-improvement books, and a sought after speaker with a client list featuring a Who's Who of leading corporations. His website is www. MarkVictorHansen.com.

Other Books by Dan Kennedy, Published by Entrepreneur Press

No B.S. Direct Marketing for NON-Direct Marketing Businesses (4th Edition)

No B.S. Trust-Based Marketing (with Matt Zagula)

No B.S. Grassroots Marketing for Local Businesses (with Jeff Slutsky)

No B.S. Price Strategy (with Jason Marrs)

No B.S. Business Success in The New Economy

No B.S. SALES Success in The New Economy

No B.S. Wealth Attraction (for Entrepreneurs) in The New Economy

No B.S. Ruthless Management of People & Profits

No B.S. Marketing to the Affluent

No B.S. Time Management for Entrepreneurs (2nd Edition)

The Ultimate Marketing Plan (4th Edition)

The Ultimate Sales Letter (4th Edition)

Making Them Believe: The 21 Principles and Lost Secrets of Dr. J.R. Brinkley-Style Marketing (with Chip Kessler)

Uncensored Sales Strategies (with Sydney Barrows)

Index

THE MOST INCREDIBLE
Free Gift EVER

Learn How to claim your $633.91 Worth of Pure,
Powerful Money-Making Information Absolutely FREE

Including a FREE "Test-Drive" of
GKIC Insider's Circle Gold Membership

All You Have To Do is Go Here Now:
www.gkic.com/brandbook

The Iron Tribe Fitness Franchise Turn-Key Business Opportunity

FREE

Over $799 Value Collection of 3 DVDs
Plus Other Resources -- for a Limited Time

Got a passion for fitness? Want to turn that passion into profits?

If so, you may qualify to own the <u>ultimate</u> lifestyle business -- as an Iron Tribe Fitness franchisee. We've gone from a 400 sq. ft. garage to more than 50 units across America in 3 years. What's the secret? Our **turn-key systems** ensure your success by giving you a clear, proven path to follow:

- **Predictable Income**, with plug-and-play systems for lead generation, new customer acquisition, and multiple recurring revenue streams. Prospects are pre-determined to join before you ever speak to them!
- **Market Researched and Protected Territories**, so you can build your business and forget about competition
- **Done-For-You Equipment and Construction Packages**, to help you ramp up to profitability fast!

To learn more about the Iron Tribe Franchising opportunity, please complete and return the form below for your **FREE Gift**. You'll receive a 3-DVD Collection of videos documenting the 11 Essential Systems of the ITF business model, location tours, marketing campaigns that pull in clients by the boatload, and a whole lot more. The value of this DVD training is $799, but it's being offered FREE to the first qualified person in your area. After your area is taken, this offer is void and must be withdrawn without notice.

Please Print Clearly to Guarantee the Delivery of Your Free DVD Collection:

Your Name: _____ Business Name: _____

Mailing Address: _____

City: _____ State: _____Zip: _____

Phone: (_____) _____ Fax: (_____) _____

Email (we do NOT believe in Spam): _____

Are you a trainer or micro gym owner currently?

_____

What are your top 3 locations choices (zips codes) for your ITF Franchise?

_____

What is your biggest stumbling block in your business at the moment? (This is confidential, so please be honest) :

_____

_____

_____

Your Signature (Required): _____ Date: _____

Submitting this form constitutes permission for us to contact you regarding these interests via mail, email, fax, phone and other devices in the future.

▼▼

4 Easy Ways To Claim Your FREE $799 DVD Collection:

1. **Scan and Email** this form to: Kelli@IronTribeFranchise.com
2. **Fax** this form back to 1-205-226-8676
3. **Call** the Office toll free at 1-855-226-8699
4. **Visit** www.IronTribeFranchise.com and fill out the online form